BU

CHARACTER CULTURE

for Trust and Results in the Workplace

KATHLEEN REDMOND

IC PUBLISHING

P25 => Culture drives outcome

P43 => What people do => competence

=> How people work together => character

P49 => Trust is a result of character & competence

Testimonials

"When it comes to organizational development, the soft stuff is the hard stuff. Culture change is the hardest of all. This book marries the wisdom of Stephen Covey with the story telling of Ken Blanchard to guide change agents through the process. Its practical suggestions make it a must-have handbook for leaders who care."

— Bob Willard, Author and Speaker
Sustainability Advantage, and former Manager, Leadership Development, IBM Canada

"This book talks about creating a healthy culture. Canada loses about thirty-three billion annually on decreased productivity due to mental health issues including anxiety and depression. Kathleen presents, in a palatable fashion, a well researched framework for a civil, respectful, high performing workplace."

— Ute Lawrence, Publisher
Mental Fitness Magazine

"I am really interested to hear what happens to Claire and her team next. This is an intriguing way to demonstrate theory and show us examples of Character in Action. I also appreciate that Kathleen has grounded the story in research which helps to make the sometimes intangible character values more tangible through her narrative structure."

— Karen Addison, Executive Director
Character Community Foundation of York Region

"Given the choice, very few of us would be opposed to working in an organization that lives and breathes a Character Culture; but, how do you get there? In *Building a Character Culture*, Kathleen lays out a step-by-step process that is easy to understand and enjoyable to read."

— Mike Chadsey, General Manager
Thornhill Golf and Country Club

"Talk about a good meal deftly and nutritiously assembled! This book drills down on key elements of leading a team within a pillars framework that addresses critical areas of leadership including accountability, engagement, communications, and innovation. In support of this Kathleen outlines a set of Character Values that are essential in the building of the pillars for team and individual success."

— John Walker, MBA
Education Management Consultant

"Everyone can relate to this story whether past, present, or future. Creating a story line to exemplify a coaching culture is brilliant. It's practical, grounded in research, and relevant for today's leaders."

— Judy Montaigne, Manager
Government of Ontario

"Kathleen is the queen of insight and common sense in tackling the epic battle between character and culture. It is a battle that is more urgent than ever in our business world today. She has wrapped an easy to read story of a complex situation with leading edge concepts that marry character and culture plus she has 'put a bow on the package' by supporting these tough topics with practical insights and useful tools. This is more than a book—it is a compendium with a powerful story, well researched insights, and practical tools—all between the covers of *Building a Character Culture*.

Digging deeper, the reader will notice that Kathleen brings to life the danger and power of playing the trust card which is central to the Character Culture debate. As her well documented research to the story illustrates, business owners and managers worldwide are being challenged to rise above the traditional business mentality of 'give-the-customers-whatever-they-want-so-long-as-it-makes-a-profit.' But can business owners make the transition? Her approach is neither quick nor easy to do. To make it work requires fresh tools and a fresh approach.

Building a Character Culture starts with a story that takes the reader on an emotional roller coaster ride. La Maison is the setting, where guests relax and enjoy interesting food and look out over a beautiful park, while the staff are in a state of turmoil triggered by the death of the owner. The central character, Claire, is charged with dealing with the mess. She is slammed with issue after issue. Will Claire have the character to take on the prevailing culture and introduce a new way of thinking or will she default to the traditional business mentality? Will she show that, despite the odds, she is open to using the new tools of engagement? Can Claire move quickly enough to both save the business yet take the time to understand the needs of this immediate community and provide the 'fresh air' so necessary for trust to nurture and grow? Bottom line—how will Claire play the trust card?

There is so much 'beef' in this compendium that I found it needed a third reading to digest it all. This book is definitely a keeper!"

— Stuart Morley, MBA
The MBO Group Inc., Acquisition Specialists

"The Character Pillars and Values provide a succinct model for employee success, the creation of a winning team and the ability to change how an organization conducts business. In her usual style, Kathleen provides, through a great story, easy steps to follow when introducing a Character Culture in a business environment. This innovative guide is a true winner!"

— Virginia Hackson, Mayor
Town of East Gwillimbury

"The situation rings very true! It is a very believable situation with the realities of change and the fear that informs the atmosphere; realistic presentation of the dilemma of the leader and the approach to engagement. And it is all presented in the context of the 'art of the possible' and the discipline and integrity that must inform these tough turnarounds."

— Ross Roxburgh
Principal, Roxburgh Consulting

"Kathleen has such a great way of making well researched information and strategies feel practical. My team is always able to implement what we learn from her, whether in workshops, coaching sessions, her books, or on the job."

— Lisa Alexander, Director
Learning & People Development, Extreme Brandz Group of Companies

First published in Canada by I C Publishing 2013

Library and Archive Canada Cataloguing in Publication

Building a Character Culture
Kathleen Redmond
Paperback ISBN: 978-0-9917530-7-9
e-book: 978-0-9917530-8-6
e-reader: 978-0-9917530-9-3

Publishing: I C Publishing
Design: WeMakeBooks.ca

Printed in Canada
ICpublishing.ca

For my beloved aunt, **Irene Margaret Kennedy** (1915–2008). Her unconditional love was one of the blessings of my life.

Table of Contents

Foreword

It is not surprising how preoccupied corporations and businesses are with profits, goals, objectives, and all of the other important challenges that will measure and impact their success. These preoccupations are natural, given that there is so much pressure to succeed in the business world.

Yet, businesses and their managers sometimes overlook the importance of how they do business: values and character-building practices often take a back seat. This oversight has serious negative consequences, both for the organization which may never achieve its potential, and for its employees whose contributions and abilities may not be fully realized. Appreciating what good character practices can contribute to the growth and performance of a business represents a new way of doing business.

Kathleen Redmond's penetrating and thoughtful insights present how a value- and character-centred organization will accomplish even greater achievements. Kathleen is a modern thinker who uses practical examples and straightforward strategies to demonstrate how to implement a character-informed business headed for success.

When you realize how fundamental and powerful a character culture business can be, you will wonder why you did not start a program like this before.

W. Donald Cousens, L.L.D. (1938–2017)
Former MPP of the Ontario Legislature
Former Mayor of Markham, Ontario, Canada

Preface

Clients tell me daily about their workplace reality. They are continually challenged to lead successfully with authenticity and integrity, while at the same time creating a culture that supports organizational effectiveness. *Building a Character Culture for Trust and Results in the Workplace* is a bridge to serve their reality with well substantiated, useful solutions. Theory is necessary but powerful, practical tools to apply the theory are what really count.

This book is written in a very different style from my first two books, *Rules of Engagement for Communicating at Work* (2003), and *Leadership by Engagement* (2008). The goal is that the story creates "Edutainment"; that the characters remind you of familiar people and circumstances.

The story and the characters are an amalgam of the experiences of many different clients I have coached and supported over the past thirty plus years. It has been an interesting and exciting experience to put into words, the challenges, pitfalls, passions, and successes that leaders experience daily. The Executive Coach in my story presents a process and direction, based on experience and research. We all know, however, that there have been many paths to success. Organizations, like people, are all different and you will have to find your own path and do what feels right for you.

Thanks to Aprille Janes for teaching me to write the dialogue in a way that may be of interest to you, the reader. Thanks also to Dr. Julie Reid, an expert in leadership development, for the passionate discussions and contributing to Part Two, The Evidence.

As a graduate program university instructor in the Masters of Leadership program at the University of Guelph, a certified Executive Coach (International Coach Federation), and a person who learns every day from my clients, I truly hope that this book and the tools serve you well.

Acknowledgements

May I please acknowledge,

My clients. I learn from you every day. There are many courageous, generous, fair people who are prepared to do the hard work of creating and sustaining a Character Culture. May this book honour your aspirations!

Sheri Andrunyk, Kim Leitch and the team at I C Publishing. You are thorough, well informed and encouraging.

Rosanne Wild. Your insight, wisdom, and support are invaluable. Keep up that candour!

The generous people who have read the book and offered precious feedback: Stuart Morley, Virginia Hackson, Lois Tori, Rick Dominico, Don Cousens, Bob Willard, Karen Addison, and Ute Lawrence.

Thanks to Dan Ruby of York Region and Karen Dubeau of the Newmarket Chamber of Commerce for providing opportunities for leaders to learn and flourish.

Michael Chadsey for the "office" vision, Sandra Pickard for your historical insights, and John Walker for reviewing the restaurant logistics.

Steve Risavy and Amanda Feiler. Your research into the Character Culture Framework is so important. It is critical that this model supports a healthy, effective workplace.

My own little network of long term friends and informal advisers: Patrick McCann, Trish Hewitt, Scott Murray, Roland Lange and Peggy Grall.

I must mention my husband, Terry Russell, for his patience and encouragement. No matter how much I aim to write during work time, there is inevitably spillover into evenings, very early mornings and weekends. Thank you for your unfailing sense of humour and support.

With gratitude,

Kathleen

Introduction

Building a Character Culture for Trust and Results in the Workplace is the first in the La Maison du Parc series. Through a story about a restaurant, it presents many of the challenging situations that my clients face every day, identifies the problems in a clear manner, and follows up with supporting research and practical tools. The book introduces the Character Culture Framework which underpins all the stories.

Part One—The Story. You will read about a young woman who inherits from a beloved uncle, a restaurant that needs healthy, engaging leadership. She hires an Executive Coach who supports her and her team with a process that begins by assessing their current culture. The assessment provides valuable information that helps the organization build a plan to leverage their strengths and tackle areas of opportunity in order to thrive—for the benefit of their guests, staff, and the greater community.

Part Two—The Evidence. Research that will be integral to the entire La Maison du Parc series is presented within the context of the Character Culture Framework. Understanding people and behaviour, however, is an evolving process, and the Framework will undoubtedly also evolve over time with new research, experiences, and learnings.

Part Three—The Tools. A number of practical tools, which also stem from the research, are applied in the story and outlined for you, the reader, in order to demonstrate how they could be used in your organization.

Part One

The Story:
La Maison du Parc

Chapter One

The Announcement

This is the most important decision of my life. My future hangs in the balance. The surprise that stunned me last month has changed everything. This morning's meeting is a turning point for the staff, the business, and me. It's time.

The well-worn stairs creak as I descend from the top floor office to the second level dining room which doubles as conference space. The scents of baking bread and sautéing onions waft through the stately old red brick house. The gentle chink of china and glass announce lunch preparations below.

Coffee, muffins, and fruit wait on the buffet in one corner of the room and a blank flip chart on an easel is in the other. I remove the extra seats to ensure an unbroken circle for the managers. Three padded arm chairs comfortably surround the well-polished table. Spring air ripples the lace curtains and perfumes the room.

Images from the last four weeks glide through my mind. First was the surprising meeting with Uncle Charles' executor who explained that the business and building are bequeathed to me, Claire Gilbert, his eldest niece, with a stipend for specific use. Then I took a leave of absence from my job to spend the next weeks talking with staff, observing the restaurant, chatting with guests, talking to the managers, and wrestling with this decision.

I discovered Uncle Charles' early journals in his third floor living area adjacent to his office. He kept them as faithfully as a captain's log. In 1976, he returned from a year backpacking in

Europe where he had experienced an epiphany. Dining in Europe was entirely different than anything he'd known in Toronto.

He was born a couple of years after the end of World War II and his food experience was limited to fish and chip shops, Chinese restaurants, the formal Arcadian Court, Shopsy's on Spadina, and the greasy abundance of the Canadian National Exhibition. His family dined out once a year at either a downtown Italian restaurant or in China Town. The "rich" people dined in private clubs, out of sight, access, and budget of ordinary folk.

Eating was one of the tasks of the day. Food was hastily prepared, ample enough to feed farm hands, quickly consumed, and the cleanup was often longer than the meal.

His dream was to create a place where people could relax, pay attention to well prepared, interesting food, and enjoy the beauty of the park. He was ahead of his time by asking the chef to use local foods as much as possible in our Canadian climate. Staff was trained in the origin of the food, ingredients, and preparation. Attention was paid to attractive presentation.

He enjoyed restoring the old mansion to its original Victorian elegance, choosing furniture that was functional and fit the time period. Glass pieces were also carefully selected. Several pieces of his mother's cranberry glass graced the dining rooms. Hamilton's Sovereign Potters created quality tableware and supplied the original china.

He envisioned a core staff that worked full time at La Maison du Parc, would perceive hospitality as a viable professional choice, and earn a good living too, which would allow them to buy homes, raise families, and enjoy full lives. These people would be on salary and have benefits. Charles believed that the hospitality industry in Europe was granted more respect than the Canadian perception of a transient and entry level business.

(How the world has changed! Now chefs are rock stars and we are so much more knowledgeable and interested in food and dining.)

I was touched to read that during the summers I waitressed he noticed both my interest in food and my desire to please guests. At the time I had no idea of his thoughts and feelings. I regretted not getting to know him better.

Ultimately the journals described the restaurant as, "a business where local people could dine on well prepared, good quality food at reasonable prices, in a beautiful setting, while being respectfully and well attended."

Several things really stood out in these past few weeks. The staff, many of whom have been at La Maison for years, are truly grieving Uncle Charles' passing. He was the head, heart, and soul of the business. Even the second floor office tenant, Gene LeBrun, is in mourning. He and my uncle were friends from university days. I had met Gene socially over the years and knew that he rented space for his Executive Coaching practice. The stipend related to Gene. My uncle left a letter asking that Gene support the business over the next year until things stabilized.

Secondly, the current feel of the restaurant concerned me. I remembered something different when I waitressed and visited throughout the years. Staff enjoyed working here, as did I. The dining rooms were filled with the clink and rustle of people being served and relishing a meal. Conversation and laughter percolated throughout the whole house. Now periods of tense silence replace that lighter feeling. Guests often watch the staff rather than pay attention to what's going on at their table.

Finally, the three senior managers don't seem to work together nor include the supervisors in leadership decisions and activities.

"Do I stay or do I go?" I can almost hear the thumping music from *Chicago* accompanying the question that echoes in my mind.

One by one the managers arrive. First Connie, Front of House Manager, formal in her tailored navy blue suit and crisp white blouse, enters with a nod. I'm always surprised at her small stature yet robust presence. Next to appear is Paul, the Controller, texting as he walks in. He's wearing his ever present golf shirt and khaki pants. Nicolas, the Executive Chef, in his kitchen whites, rushes in carrying a clipboard and mechanical pencil. His shaved head is shiny, no doubt from the heat of the kitchen.

They pour coffee and take a seat around the table. Paul and Nicolas are both absorbed in their own worlds of cell phone and inventory.

I get to my feet and take a deep breath before picking up the serious, thick black marker, and print three lines on the sand coloured paper:

- Announce decision
- Listen to all perspectives
- Agree on next steps

Out of the corner of my eye I see Paul put down his cell phone and lean forward. Connie sits bolt upright. Nicolas leans back in his chair and waits. I set my glasses on the table with a silent vow not to fiddle with them.

"I want to thank you for taking the time to answer my questions and allowing me to observe the restaurant for the last few weeks. It's admirable how you continued during this difficult period. There have been no issues with customers or suppliers from what I understand."

I take a deep breath. *Here goes the rest of my life. I actually gave notice at my work two weeks ago, which is why I have recently been here evenings and weekends. There is no going back.*

"As you know, it was a surprise Uncle Charles left me La Maison du Parc. That said, it seems urgent for me to step in even though the paperwork isn't final. I've decided to do so; and simply assume his role, which was owner. We all know this business is somewhat new to me, although I worked here as a young woman and leadership skills are transferable. Still, I'm asking for your support to create a dynamic and productive team, which I'll lead. I'm absolutely prepared to put my resources and energy into making this business even more successful than it already is."

It seems the air has been sucked out of the room. Three sets of eyes fix on me. The old, padded chair squeaks as I sit down and wait for what will be said next.

Paul clacks his coffee cup on the table and straightens the teaspoon.

"With all due respect Claire, this is a tough business and you have absolutely no experience with restaurants. I know you worked for a large organization but I can't imagine anything more different from this. You need to be realistic. I've been running La Maison for the last year."

I almost bite my tongue with a desire to respond but I had promised myself that I wouldn't debate with anyone. The "large organization" comment sounds like an insult. My role was to research, write learning programs, and facilitate leadership development across our country. But I don't contest. I'm here to listen.

"Paul, I am grateful for your candour." I pick up my pen to note what he, and everyone else has to say. "What about the rest of you? What are your thoughts?"

Connie is still sitting ramrod straight in her chair, and adds, "It seems you're going to do what you want no matter what we say."

As she turns to Paul I glimpse a line of perspiration on her upper lip. "You need to speak up for all of us. This isn't right."

Paul shakes his head in mild disgust as I swivel to look at Nicolas.

Chef places his clipboard on the table with a gentle smack. "I just want the freedom to run my kitchen. Make sure I get what I need and I actually don't care about titles."

I believe him, or maybe just want to believe anything remotely positive at this point.

My objective was to tell them my decision and get a sense of their reactions. Mission accomplished. Even if there isn't total support, I know where I stand.

"Well, I appreciate your time this morning. This week is booked for me to organize my office, create a learning plan so I'm familiar with every position, and dive into the financial details. Let's meet later this week and finalize our strategies. Thank you, and have a good day everyone."

The three hurriedly take their leave.

I look through the ochre and blue stained glass accented window at the beautiful grounds. The view of the huge pond which we share with the neighbouring park calms me, as always. The Toronto skyscrapers are hidden year-round which contributes to this sense of peace.

I wonder what the summer harvest will yield. I hope this is the right decision. There's so much at stake. I'd give my eye teeth to hear the conversations taking place below as I return to the third floor. In the meantime, this evening is something to look forward to. My stalwart friends and informal advisory committee are meeting me in our favourite downtown bistro. Teesha, Hal and Ping always offer support, common sense, and an interesting perspective to any conversation.

Chapter Two

The Reaction

Paul and Nicolas head to the kitchen that suggests simmering garlic, onion, butter, and white wine.

Paul launches, "This is ridiculous but it won't go on too long. She needs me and I won't make this easy. Charles strung me along with implications that I'd be in control someday."

"Your salary stays the same. What's the difference? You just deal with Claire instead of Charles," Nicolas replies.

"The point is I thought I'd get the top job. Now we have someone parachuted in to train." Paul shakes his head. "This is crap."

Nicolas moves toward the stove. "We open in two hours. I have to get things going. Let's get through lunch and talk later today."

Paul shrugs and stomps to his small office next to the kitchen.

Connie is sitting in her corner of the Supervisor's office staring out the large window overlooking the brownish green herb garden.

"She has no idea what she's getting into," Connie says into the telephone as she turns to flip through the reservation log. "I liked and trusted Charles but she has a lot to prove to me. I'll call you later tonight and tell you the whole story."

Laura, the bookkeeper, looks up from her desk in the opposite corner and shakes her head as Connie marches towards the front of the house. She picks up the phone and dials four numbers.

"Paul, it's Laura. It's only fair to give her the letter. This could change everything and we can't hold off. If you won't do it, I will." Laura takes the official looking document out of her desk and heads out to find Claire.

Paul intercepts her at the bottom of the stairs. “I’ll take it to her. I want to see the look on her face.” Laura shrugs, hands him the envelope, and heads back to her desk.

Chapter Three

The Surprise

I hear quick steps on the stairs.

Paul doesn't sit, just stands in the doorway holding an envelope. "This arrived a couple of weeks ago. You're the boss, so here you go." He tosses the envelope on my desk and watches me open it. I feel a knot forming in my stomach. Blunt words state that we're six months behind on the second mortgage and the new owner must call the mortgagor, a local lawyer, immediately.

"Paul," I stammer, "how long have you known mortgage payments are in arrears?"

"Charles always dealt with the lawyers, so I'm not entirely sure of the arrangement. Of course I know we don't have the cash for the payments."

"Why didn't you tell me?" I am incredulous at this news.

"You didn't ask," he smirks.

"I certainly did ask you about our financial situation," I retort, running both hands through my thick red hair which suddenly feels hot and sticky.

"If you'd really looked at the P & L you'd have known. You didn't seem interested in the details." Paul turns on his heels and jogs down the stairs.

I sit stunned, take off my glasses, and shake my head. What do I do now?

When I look up, the tenant, Gene, has replaced Paul in the doorway. Even in my current state I notice that he looks well groomed and professional. Crisp white shirt, sharply creased pants, good belt, and a black, white-tipped pen in his pocket.

Seems to be the new, more casual uniform for businessmen these days.

"Rough day?" he inquires carefully from the doorway.

"Yes, the last couple of days have been quite challenging. Thanks for asking."

"Mind if I sit down for a moment?"

I nod and he eases himself into the wingback chair across from the old desk.

"You're catching me at a tough moment," I succeed in saying.

"I guessed that from the speed of the traffic on the stairs," Gene responds with a lift of his eyebrow.

"How much did my uncle talk to you about the business?"

"I do know the business is struggling and you've assumed responsibility. I know that he wants me to support La Maison through the transition, in whatever manner you choose. As a grizzled long-time leader who now serves as a business coach, you can talk to me if it helps. Nothing could ever surprise me and everything is private."

I am talking to him a bit earlier than I imagined, but at this point it feels like there is nothing left to lose. I'm not sure if it's because my uncle wants him to help us, or I have known him forever, but I move to close the door. As I turn back to him, words pour out.

"You probably know much of this, but here is my perspective. My uncle had a successful business which is at risk. If the worst happens, his legacy is completely lost. The managers range from toleration to rejecting me completely. Revenue is slipping and we are losing our guest base. I just read a letter from a lawyer, Lou Baines, telling me that we're behind in our mortgage payments and risk foreclosure. I left a good job, the promise of a pension, and benefits for a more uncertain future than I realized. My family's angry that I inherited the business. They believe I won a lottery. To say that I am somewhat overwhelmed is an understatement."

Gene simply listens and nods. Telling him seems to help, especially as my trio of supporters are still a few hours away. And they question me for forfeiting a secure, well-paying position to work constantly so "supporters" may not quite describe their role.

After a brief pause, Gene quietly asks, "What feels most urgent?"

"The mortgage payments! The building and the business will disappear unless this gets sorted out. What can I do?"

"What do you want to do?" Gene asks in a calm, even voice.

"I need to buy some time. I don't have the cash to pay what's outstanding and I don't know if the business has any money."

"So what's your first step in buying time?" he continues.

"Well, I must understand our financial situation and it's muddy until the will is probated and everything is finalized. In the meantime, we need to determine how much money can be allocated to back payments," I say without giving it much thought.

"So, it sounds like you need information and a plan before contacting the lawyer?" Gene clarifies.

"Yes, absolutely, and I want to contact him today. If not, I'll be awake all night worrying."

"Staying awake is definitely not going to help. How will you get the information you need?" Gene continues.

"Well, Paul has the most complete financial information. Plus I have to confront him about his behaviour, which feels disrespectful and unprofessional."

"So, it sounds like you need a bit of time to talk to Paul and then call the lawyer. What will stop you from taking these steps this afternoon?"

"Nothing at all; this is truly urgent," I respond.

"What will be the first thing you'll do after I take my leave?" he smiles as he stands.

"Call Paul up here and not let him go until I have what I need. No more vague and snide answers."

"How difficult is this for you right now? You say you're a bit rattled by this news." Gene asks.

I close my eyes for a moment, checking in with myself. "Good point. I should take a few minutes and gather my thoughts; maybe list the information I need." I pull a pad of paper towards myself and pick up a pen. "Gene, this has been incredibly helpful and the timing is eerie. Thanks for your advice."

"You're welcome, but I offered no advice. I simply asked some basic coaching questions to help you think through this challenge and clarify next steps. You did the heavy lifting," Gene states with a smile that warms his brown eyes.

My next words surprise even me. "Gene, I would appreciate some objective guidance. Are you aware that my uncle left monies for you to support the business after his passing?"

"Yes, he told me, but I want to assure you that you must do what you believe to be right for yourself and the business. Having said that, I would be delighted to support you. What do you need?"

I tap my pen on the pad of paper as I think about my answer. "I need a plan. Also, someone I trust to get me going in the right direction and help maintain momentum."

"Claire, it would be my pleasure. Let's schedule an hour tomorrow to roll up our sleeves and clarify specifically what you want to achieve and how we might work together," Gene states.

"I need to totally understand how we would work together, if that is our decision," I respond.

"Of course, that's imperative. Tomorrow, let's start working on your objectives. When we are really clear, and if you think my services would be helpful, I can draft a service agreement. You can review it in detail before we proceed."

I nod as Gene leaves the office. I take five minutes to sketch out the information I need, then pick up the phone and call Paul.

Chapter Four

A Watershed Moment

Paul enters, talking. His ear bud resembles a Star Trek parasite protruding from the right side of his head. His short, gelled hair adds to the illusion of a strange, intergalactic creature. This look doesn't improve his brittle thinness. I motion him to sit across from me at the desk.

"Paul, how did we get behind on the mortgage payments?" I ask, trying to neither grit my teeth nor appear tense.

"Charles lost sight of what was going on," he blames immediately. Clearly taking responsibility is not his area of strength.

"How does the system work? Tell me how the finances are actually managed."

"Bills come in and Laura logs the payables. Every day the revenues are entered. Once a month we pay the bills," Paul lists.

"Who's actually in control of the money? Ensures that money goes into the bank, everything is up to date and signs the cheques?"

"I do. With Laura's help," he confirms.

"So what happened with the mortgage payments?" My clenched jaw is starting to hurt.

"When things got tight I took the bills to Charles and he decided what to pay. He told me he would ask for an extension. Next thing he's in the hospital and I don't know what arrangement has been made. Then this letter arrives. You were already here and announced you're the new boss. Simple as that." Paul eyes me coldly but at least he pulls out that damn ear bud.

"It seems reasonable to assume that Charles didn't call the lawyer. What is our current financial situation?"

"We're just breaking even without the second mortgage payments."

"How much money can we put towards back payments? We need a plan to start paying off the arrears."

He crosses one leg over the other, apparently relishing this. "Pulling out more money will be tough, but we're going into the summer season. We've more revenue from the patio. If we really watch costs we can squeeze out an extra six thousand per month. That would pay the arrears by the end of the year. I have no idea if it'll fly, but it's the best I can do."

"What do you see as the alternative?"

Paul shrugs, flicking an imagined piece of lint off his knee. "Sell the business or let me run it. We save the salary you're no doubt going to demand and we're up to date in four months." At this point, with my job gone, my loyalty to my uncle as well as my pride on the line, there is no way either alternative will be considered, not for one second.

"I'll call the lawyer. Wait here so we can finish our conversation."

I pick up the phone. Paul punches a number into his cell but stays put.

The lawyer answers on the first ring, which surprises me in this day of voicemail. The second surprise is that Lou is a woman. I rapidly reconfigure my vision of this person.

"Lou, please accept my apology," my opening gambit after a brief introduction. "I just found out about the arrears."

"Claire, I knew your uncle for a long time and was sorry to hear of his death. This is the first time that La Maison du Parc is in this situation. What's going on?"

"It appears things slipped in the last few months. I absolutely commit to getting us get back on track, starting today." I look pointedly at Paul, who ignores me.

"We can help sell the business if you can't run it successfully. And you can always sell the building. You should realize a small profit from it."

"Lou, I have every intention of ensuring La Maison gets on her feet and stays that way." The phone now feels slippery in my palms. "I propose that we start paying off the arrears next month."

"How long until you're up to date?" is the icy reply.

"Worst case scenario, January 1 of next year."

"If the entire arrears isn't paid off by then, you must understand I'll start foreclosure proceedings on January 2. Agree to those terms and you have your eight months."

Now I just feel sick in every way possible. I can't see another choice.

"Done," I respond as firmly as my voice permits.

"Good, I'll courier a written agreement to you by the end of the week."

Lou hangs up the phone without a good bye. I take a deep breath and try to calm my roiling insides.

"Paul, we've bought time so that's the good news."

He nods but stays silent, forcing me to continue. "I need to talk to you about working together. The late information and your approach to this serious issue is inappropriate and frankly surprising. And your demeanour with me is unacceptable. What's going on?"

He uncrosses his legs and leans forward, his face reddening. "I didn't sign on to have you as my boss. As the new owner, this is your responsibility, not mine."

"So, you're telling me that it won't work with me in this role?"

"You have to give all of us time to adjust," he answers.

"What is different, other than you're reporting to me rather than Charles?"

Paul almost spits the next words, "Charles understood the business. You don't."

I struggle to keep my voice calm. "Paul, here's what I need from you. A commitment to thoroughly answer my questions with as much detail as I ask. Respectful behaviour in any and every situation, which means you don't threaten, put down, or make any comment that's a slight. If you have feedback for me, ask my permission first. Will you do that?"

He studies his fingers as he drums the arm of his chair for a moment. The moment seems to go on forever. Finally he looks up and meets my eyes, the challenge clear in his. "What choice do I have?"

"You have complete choice. You chose to work here and you can choose to continue working here, knowing this expectation. It's up to you."

"Are you threatening to fire me?" He moves forward in his seat as though to stand.

"I'm clarifying my expectation of you. Given the situation let's go to the bank tomorrow and I'll assume signing authority until everything is on track. It is important for me to trust our systems and for the staff to trust me. Hopefully they know that I am of good character. Trust is the fruit of both competence and character so I plan to work in every position in the restaurant to build my competence as quickly as possible. I would like to start with your job, beginning tomorrow mid-morning. Do I have your commitment to work together in this professional manner?"

Now he does stand. "Fine."

I stand as well, feeling it's important to stay level with him. "Paul, I'm hopeful you'll stay and that we will work together effectively. It's up to you."

As the door closes behind him, I make a note of the conversation and lock the file folder in my desk.

Definitely time to leave and meet my friends.

We've been close since we all worked together years ago. The little, intimate bistro is still quiet in the early evening. Teesha is already at our corner table. Her professional role is vice president, human resources for an international publishing company. She greets me with a smile and a hug. Soon Hal joins us. He works as an employment lawyer in a downtown firm, and will return to work after dinner. Finally Ping arrives. His job as director of operations for a large quick service food company often requires him to travel. We know it's a treat to be together.

I catch them up and they toast my new life. Teesha encourages me to work with Gene, as her company has experienced good results with executive coaches. Hal reminds me to thoroughly document critical conversations with staff. Ping's words of wisdom are to take care of myself every step of the way. They all promise to help any way they can. And dine often at La Maison du Parc.

Chapter Five

Coaching Commences

The next morning Gene and I meet early in the conference room. The large bay windows face the park and the water. It wasn't a great night sleep-wise, but I do feel better, especially after some laughs and good food with my friends. A flip chart page waits on the wall. The easel has disappeared but those sticky pages are handy. I make a mental note to make sure the marker doesn't bleed through to the wallpaper. No additional costs!

"I know you want a plan. Let's start in the classic way, with the end in mind," he opens the conversation. "Determine a future date and what's happening to the business. Describe it in as much detail as you can."

Movement on the pond catches my eye. The ice is almost melted and the gorgeous white swans are back. The black and orange of their beaks is just visible from this distance. No wonder Uncle Charles loved this place.

"Right now I can't think past January of next year," I reply turning back to Gene. "Ok, here's a start. All the bills are paid, the holiday season was busy and profitable, the leaders are supportive and pulling in the same direction, the staff's doing a great job, and guests are thrilled by the food, atmosphere, and service."

"Tell me why this comes to mind for you?" Gene looks genuinely intrigued.

"Well, the financial situation is top of mind. Something must have changed, as the business was running well prior to the last few years. And whatever it is must be affecting guests. We should be deeply aware of how our guests evaluate their experience. Our success is determined by our guests' reactions and thereby, our reputation."

"What determines guest experience?" Gene asks.

"The behaviour of our staff. Whether it's a sous chef creating a dish for the hundredth time or a host greeting a party of twelve people five minutes before closing, every dish, drink, clean bathroom, and conversation counts. And my observations tell me that we aren't the restaurant we used to be," I respond.

"So you're saying you want to be absolutely certain that you are choosing the way everything works. That you want to proactively choose the culture, rather than letting things just happen?"

"Definitely. It was a different place to work years ago, and I imagine it feels like a different place to visit." Something clicks into place as we talk. It's true, it does feel very different.

"Claire, in your previous job did you ever do anything regarding workplace culture?" Gene asks.

I nod. "Yes, come to think of it. We hired a consultant to help us understand the current culture and gaps between what we wanted the culture to be."

"Was it informative?" he asks.

"As I recall it was incredibly informative. We realized why there were significant difficulties."

"What was going on?"

I feel a little thrill of discovery. His questions are jogging my memory. "We realized that the system itself stopped people from being effective. There was little accountability. It was more along the lines of, 'protect yourself, and just survive until retirement.' It was a shame because many people worked hard, but often the effort didn't really produce anything tangible. It was really discouraging."

"What happened in the end?" Gene continued.

"The consultant wrote a plan to bridge the gaps, but nothing really changed."

"Was someone senior championing the plan?"

"In name, but at arm's length. Lots of time and effort was spent, but nothing came of it," I respond. I remembered all the time I had spent facilitating focus groups, and listening to staff and clients. Ultimately we squandered money and created staff disappointment.

"Ok, so let's think about this for a minute. You're concerned about the culture of La Maison, particularly in light of the financial difficulties, which means the business isn't performing as well as it can. You had some experience with different workplace cultures. What does all this mean for you at this point?"

Gene gives me very few answers but certainly seems to be asking the right questions. Why hadn't I put these pieces together for myself? Every organization has a culture. And it's critical to the success of the organization to understand the culture. People behave differently in other cultures. I think about the way the staff acts at a Five Star Luxury Hotel vs. No Name Motel. I know culture drives outcome. This realization is actually exciting as I can do something about it.

"Gene, yes, the culture does bear investigation. My first instinct is to get everyone to work harder, tighten belts, and keep our nose to the grindstone as a reaction to the pressure. We'll have to do that, but let's make sure we're doing the right things for the right reason and measuring our progress."

"What do you mean, 'do the right things?'" Gene asks.

"People can work incredibly hard and ultimately produce very little that counts. It's frustrating for them and puts the organization in jeopardy. I think we all, including me, need to step back and make sure we're headed in the right direction so we end up in the right place."

"It sounds like stepping back and thinking about how you define 'right things' is important. Besides being financially viable, what's important to you?" Gene asks as he pulls out his notebook and pen.

"You are right. I've barely allowed myself to consider what's really important to me. What kind of leader I want to be. I was thinking about this when trying to decide to take over my uncle's role, and then got swept up in the financial situation." I stand and walk to the window. *Of course it is time to stop and get in touch with what matters to me and do what I have always hoped is possible.*

"Gene, obviously I want the restaurant to be successful, but there is something bigger at stake for me. I know we are beyond believing that profit is the only indicator of success. We can't be successful by exploiting anyone. We must be a good citizen in our community and pay attention to our environmental impact. I believe people have incredible potential and that wise leaders tap talent for the good of the organization as well as the individual.

Also, in Canada, I believe we have an extraordinary opportunity with people from so many backgrounds who can help us understand the world more deeply and accurately, which is a benefit on all levels.

Moreover, we need to communicate robustly. Typically there is more information available than reaches the ears of decision makers.

I need leaders to be courageous, to clearly describe expectations, and offer candid, accurate feedback to support the success of others. It's important we hold each other accountable for commitments, and that we learn to work together to really create a dynamic, innovative workplace. It's also vital to have this workplace described as trustworthy and functional, a place where people enjoy working, know how to work through challenges, and are totally engaged in the success of the business and each other. And I want to be sure that we do all this by honouring Uncle Charles, his vision, and the history of La Maison," I say turning to look at Gene as I sit back down. I rather forgot about him while all of these gut level thoughts were pouring out without filter or edit.

"Claire, what you are describing is very important. Do you believe it's achievable?" Gene asks while rolling the marker gently between his fingers.

"Well, I wish I had a roadmap," I answer with a smile.

"You started by clearly describing how you want the year to end. Then you articulated what's important to you, what you value; the 'what' you want to achieve, and 'how' people must work together to achieve it. It also sounds like in January of next year you'll reassess and aim for the next step, the next 'what'." Gene walks toward the flip chart paper patiently waiting on the wall. "Are you ready to develop some concrete objectives and think about how I can be of service?"

"Yes, but do you have time to continue tomorrow? I'm meeting with Paul and then apprenticing as host. I also need to write an agenda for Friday's management meeting." I stand to leave and Gene gathers our notes. Gene agrees to meet me late tomorrow afternoon before the dinner hour.

Chapter Six

Over Poulet Maison

In the kitchen, Nicolas eyes the braising chicken. The sauce is thick, rich brown, and the delicious aroma consistent with the countless times he's prepared Poulet Maison.

Paul arrives and takes a quick, perfunctory look at the huge stainless steel pan steaming on the stove. The quantity holds more interest for him than the effort put into it or the quality of the dish.

"She's meeting with Gene again. What the hell are these two up to?" Paul launches.

"Did you read the agenda for Friday's meeting? Two items: update regarding our financial situation and discussion regarding future plans. Maybe he's helping her prepare," Nicolas says while continuing to focus on the big black gas stove.

"No, I didn't have time to read it," Paul replies.

"Well it was sent a few minutes ago," Nicolas says as he adds beurre manié to thicken the sauce.

Connie enters the kitchen with the daily schedule and reservation log in her hands.

"More email and yet another meeting," Connie utters, picking up on their conversation.

"We used to complain about not knowing what was going on. Now are you complaining about hearing what's happening?" Nicolas turns back to the stove and sautés a huge skillet of bok choy. His wiry, well-muscled 5'10" frame serves him well in this physically demanding job.

Connie turns abruptly and struts towards the dining room.

"Complaining Connie. What else is new? I'm more concerned about that redhead who replaced Charles," Paul whips back.

Nicolas stacks plates as he advises Paul, "Look, we have a meeting and an agenda. Read the damn thing. Don't worry about Connie. You know she's always angry unless you agree with her. Just leave it alone for now. Right now I want to make sure everything is ready for lunch."

Paul shakes his head and walks to his office as Nicolas gets back to work.

Chapter Seven

Character Culture Framework

"Claire, ready to create those objectives?" Gene asks the next afternoon in the conference room.

I sit in one of the big, padded chairs, pour a glass of water and realize that getting to the point quickly is a must.

"Absolutely, but first let me get it all straight. Here is what I know. One. We're in financial trouble and must start running a more profitable restaurant immediately. Two. It's imperative to understand how things really work around here, which means understanding the current culture, as the culture drives the business. I know I have some significant hopes. And three, we should create a plan that encompasses both issues in a logical, practical fashion. Can you talk about how you and I work together before we continue?" I ask.

"Alright, let's take a few minutes and clarify our arrangement. You and me. Coach and client. That information will help us create the plan," Gene says as he takes a seat beside me.

"Gene, I know that you are right. Planning is essential to success. It's just that when there's a sense of urgency like I feel right now, it's so tempting to dive in and start fixing. Ok, where do we start?" I ask.

"What if we accomplish three things in this meeting? Draft our working agreement, secondly think more about the culture, and thirdly create some first steps to get you on the path that's right for you and the business at this point in time," Gene outlines.

"Done," I respond.

"Ok, you and me. Our agreement is based on your objectives. What do you want to achieve by the end of the year, in concrete terms?" Gene asks as he stands and moves to the flip chart posted on the wall.

"I want us to be financially viable. That means that we are paying all our bills and have paid off the backlog on the second mortgage."

Gene writes this information as he turns towards me, "What can you do to ensure that financial viability is properly tracked?"

"Can you help us develop some kind of dashboard or scorecard? That would be really helpful in keeping on top of things," I say, remembering the significance of goals and tracking progress. Having said that, I haven't really seen it done well in the past.

"What if I write something like this," he explains, as he turns and writes on the flip chart.

- *Gene develops, with input from the leadership team, a scorecard that targets financial goals. Claire and Gene meet bi-weekly and update the scorecard.*

"Of course the scorecard must be developed with the leaders. They're the ones who are going to manage the costs, with me of course. What are you going to do with the results as we go along?" I ask.

"Next point: Gene coaches Claire regarding how to support results, either positive or regarding improvement," Gene states, and looks at me for confirmation.

"So you will help me figure out how to recognize improvement and manage gaps. Is that what you are saying?"

"Absolutely. Are you comfortable with me noting this?" he asks, as I nod.

"Looks like it's time to move to the next point you made when we started, assessing the culture. There's something I want to share with you based on our conversation yesterday and what's important to you," he says, and hands me a two-sided piece of paper. "This is a concept called Character Culture Framework. Rather than starting with a blank page, you can decide if this concept will give you a head start. Take a look at the concept and see what you think," Gene encourages.

Character Culture Framework – 5 Pillars

The Character Culture Framework is designed to build and sustain the trust needed to bring out the best in each person to realize the organizational purpose and achieve goals. ***The five Pillars support organizational effectiveness.***

5 Pillars	Create Clarity	Commit to Accountability
Guiding Principles **Why this Pillar is important…**	Everyone knows and understands organizational purpose, goals, progress, and results.	Everyone commits to the success of the organization by fulfilling their commitments, taking responsibility for their behaviour, and striving for excellence.
Sample Leadership behaviours **Leaders...**	Clarify organizational purpose, significance and impact Establish performance expectations Link assignments to organizational purpose Provide concrete organizational information on goals, productivity, progress and results Model and promote the Character Values Are transparent and consistent in decision-making Incorporate values into human resource systems	Hold themselves and others accountable for goals, progress and results Assess staff performance in relation to organizational goals, progress and results Assess staff behaviour in relation to the Character Culture Framework Provide appropriate tools, resources Foster and support autonomy where appropriate Are responsible to one another about commitments and behaviours
Sample behaviours for everyone (including leaders) **Everyone...**	Supports the five Pillars Models/practices Character Values Requests input/information when needed Understands what is expected	Assesses impact of their words and actions on others and on organizational goals, progress and results Self-manages by identifying intentions, thoughts and feelings which manifest in behaviour Is open to and strives for continuous improvement

Character Culture Framework Pillars—Creating the what and why foundation of a Character Culture.

Coach for Performance	Cultivate Collegiality	Collaborate for Results
Everyone supports the ongoing development of others with a focus on maximizing individual potential and organization performance.	Everyone contributes to an enjoyable workplace where they feel safe, engaged, and valued.	Everyone works collaboratively to improve the organization and achieve strategic goals.
Engage in, encourage and promote open and honest feedback in all directions Hold regular one-on-one meetings with leader, peers and direct reports Coach on performance by inquiring about intentions, thoughts and feelings which manifest in behaviour Acknowledge and celebrate progress and results Provide ongoing developmental opportunities	Establish and maintain a trusting workplace climate that promotes engagement, inclusion, caring and a sense of belonging Create awareness of the significance of body language and tone of voice in communication Clarify that technology (email, texts, voice mail etc.) is used in a careful manner. Face to face conversations are required if there is a sensitive issue	(Senior Leaders) support the "first team – the senior leadership team," as fully as their departmental teams Compromise on departmental agendas for the benefit of the organization Provide the structure and conditions to promote working together in cross-functional teams Create a simple, open to all staff, system for encouraging and harvesting innovative ideas
Offers feedback according to the agreed upon workplace protocols Communicates to leader and/or appropriate parties any opportunities to improve the organization Helps others to build their capacity to problem solve in challenging situations	Speaks up when there are opportunities for, and barriers to, collegiality and engagement Develops successful working relationships with all parties by adapting the Character Values Respects and supports diversity	Contributes to the success of the organization by taking the initiative in developing collaborative relationships with all parties, including the greater community Offers innovative suggestions for improving the organization using the system for harvesting innovative ideas

Character Culture Framework – Character Values

The Character Culture Framework integrates character and competence behaviours that are essential ingredients of trust. ***Character Values clarify how people behave in a Character Culture to develop and sustain high trust.***

Respect	Integrity
Respectful behaviour is civil, dignified, positive and inclusive.	*Behaving with integrity means being honest, responsible, fair, and consistent.*
I practice good etiquette by saying hello, goodbye, please, and thank you	I keep promises and commitments
I am punctual and let others know if and why I will be late	I tell the truth and speak from my "I" to take responsibility for words and actions
I ask people for time rather than interrupting	I ask rather than speculate on motives, thoughts, and feelings of others
I ensure others have ample opportunity to speak in conversations and meetings	I take responsibility for, and learn from, my mistakes
I am committed to the success of others, including offering developmental feedback	I strive for a win-win in all circumstances
I speak positively about my organization and colleagues	I speak directly to the person when there is a problem
I celebrate the progress and success of others	I protect the privacy of others
I use inclusive and thoughtful language and approaches with others	I explain the rationale for decisions and requests where possible
I value and learn from the differences between us	I am aware of my moods and adjust them to be collegial, collaborative, and constructive
I involve others in decision-making, discussions, and events where appropriate	I contribute to our community and society

Compassion	Courage
Being compassionate means listening actively, showing empathy, and being caring towards others.	*Being courageous means speaking up, hearing feedback, taking initiative, and optimistically persevering.*
I listen actively and openly in order to fully hear and understand what is being communicated	I state my perspective/ opinion when it seems helpful and/or is requested
I check for understanding to help ensure that I understand what others are saying and feeling	I engage in courageous conversations when appropriate and refrain from gossip
I show empathy by putting myself in the other person's shoes	I listen to feedback offered to me and discuss how to modify/adjust my approach if this is needed
I reflect the message and emotion (acknowledgement) in challenging or significant conversations	I reflect on how to improve my performance
I offer positive feedback in a generous, timely, specific manner	I am clear in my response whether the answer is "yes" or "no"
I offer developmental feedback in a constructive, open, inquiring manner that leads to a solution	I am authentic by considering my intentions, thoughts, and feelings and ensuring alignment with my behaviour
I separate the person from the issue when offering feedback	I am always assessing how to do things better and more effectively
I ask rather than tell	I go the extra mile to get the job done
I describe my own experiences as a way of providing support rather than offering advice	I seek solutions to setbacks and obstacles
I am considerate and kind	I do what is right versus popular

"Gene, I have several thoughts and a few questions," I say after carefully reading the document.

"Of course, where do you want to start?" Gene answers.

"Well, my initial thoughts are that it would be incredible to work in a place like this. This seems like what I have always hoped for."

He smiles his agreement. "As you know, no one and nowhere are perfect. Saying that, this Framework offers a model for a truly functional, high trust, effective way of working. Specific behaviours to strive towards, learn, practice, and measure."

"So the model states that clarity, accountability, coaching and supporting each other with collegiality, and collaboration are foundational for success. This sounds like my little diatribe," I quip as I stand to stretch out my back.

"Yes, and there's significant research to support that claim. Sounds like your experience tells you it's true," Gene replies.

"It makes absolute sense to me. And the Character Values of Respect, Integrity, Compassion, and Courage also seem fundamental. How are they different from the five Pillars?"

"The Pillars represent the guiding principles—what must be in place for an organization to be effective. The Character Values define how people must behave to support the guiding principles. The Character Values are fundamental to good self-management, individual leadership, and by the way, many of the laws of the land. Transforming the ideas into specific behaviours has been a significant piece of work, but helpful in clarifying expectations. It sounds like many of your ideas are mirrored on these two pages, but right now let's make sure your questions are answered," Gene responds.

"What about values that are specific to the organization? The Character Values are quite generic," I observe.

"Very insightful. Part of the process is to develop the two or three organizational values that are relevant and pertinent at a given point in time. For La Maison I would imagine that exceptional customer service is an obvious choice, for example," Gene explains as he straightens his shoulders.

"So what are you suggesting exactly?" I question.

"The thought is that we use this Framework to assess the culture of the organization. Depending on the results, you can create a plan to target the areas that require improvement."

"That makes sense. The big question, in my mind is, how do we get there?" I ask.

"There is a roadmap and I'm pleased to share it. Before I do, why don't you spend some time really digesting whether or not this description of a culture works for you? Back to our agreement. What if I write the following?" he says as he picks up the marker.

- *Administer a cultural assessment. Create a plan to leverage strengths and target specific, significant improvements.*

"I agree, and let's make the next point, 'Support Claire in coaching leaders to implement the improvement plan'," I add as Gene writes.

"Give me a couple of minutes to think this through please," Gene states as he studies the flip chart. I check emails on my cell phone. When he is ready, we both stand back and look at our agreement.

CLAIRE'S OBJECTIVES:

A. La Maison du Parc is financially viable by end of December.

Deliverables:

- Gene facilitates the development of a scorecard, with the leadership team, to create financial viability in a manner that supports people and the community.
- Gene coaches Claire to leverage strengths, support progress, and coach through gaps.

B. Transform the culture to an aspirational culture which supports financial viability and organizational success.

Deliverables:

- Gene administers The Character Culture Assessment to assess the culture of La Maison du Parc. Gene's administration includes appropriate inclusion of team members, and communication strategies as approved by Claire.
- Gene works with Claire and the leadership team to create a plan to target improvement opportunities.
- Gene leads Claire and team through the cultural transformation process.

"What do you think? Does this capture what we have discussed so far?" Gene questions.

"Totally and clearly. What is next?"

"How do we work together? This is really important." Gene sits down and takes notes in his black leather notebook. "We have some work to do upfront with the leadership team. Those meetings can be scheduled separately. What if you and I meet bi-weekly for the first three months and then monthly after that? Does that seem reasonable to you?"

"It does Gene, but please put together the costs quickly so I'm sure everything is covered without touching our cash flow. I believe this is how Uncle Charles imagined you helping me. If we can accomplish these two objectives, we will be on our way."

"What if I give you a draft agreement tomorrow? We can fill in the other pieces once all the elements are confirmed," Gene responded.

"I would like to get started working with the leaders at the meeting on Friday. Can you attend and start work on both the scorecard and explaining the Character Culture and Assessment?"

"Absolutely, and if you like we can meet for an hour tomorrow morning and answer any questions that arise for you before we share it with the leaders. Let me know if in any way it isn't right, specific, or practical enough for you. I will also show you the draft breakdown of the costs of this initiative."

"Deal," I say, and head upstairs to my office to read the Character Culture Framework in detail and think about what this could mean for us.

Chapter Eight

Preparing for the Managers' Meeting

I take a moment and enjoy the view from my office window before Gene arrives. This way we don't usurp the dining room if it's needed for lunch. Outside not only have ducks joined the swans, but baby ducks are following their mothers in straight little lines. The trees are getting fuller every day and the new growth is chartreuse and virginal. The faithful iris stalks at the base of our property on the edge of the pond are a good foot tall, strengthening to support their purple and white crowns. One of our benches sits patiently empty a couple of feet from the water. I wish I could be sitting there with a cup of coffee.

"It's beautiful on a sunny day, isn't it?" Gene comments as he enters the office.

"It's beautiful any day. It's the heart of the park and the neighbourhood. It's such a peaceful, protected place compared to our neighbouring massive, unpredictable Lake Ontario," I respond.

"Back to work," I slowly turn from the window. "Here is what I understand. A Character Culture fosters a healthy workplace where there is high trust, authentic engagement, and sustained focus on organizational purpose."

"That is spot-on Claire. And the Character Culture Framework provides people with a clear picture of what a Character Culture looks like in an organization. It describes what people do (competence) and how they work together (character) irrespective of roles and responsibilities. It is a resource that organizations can use to foster a healthy workplace characterized by high trust, authentic engagement and sustained focus on organizational purpose."

"Excellent! Now I'd like to know a little more about how we get there. What are the steps in this process? This must mean that we will go through a cultural transformation. I want to understand it completely before we present it to the leaders."

"There are six key steps to transforming to a Character Culture, which in essence means ensuring clarity of purpose and providing supportive behaviour. The steps appear straight forward but the actual process, which means involving people, can be a bit messy," Gene explains.

"Fine, let's get started."

"Why don't you get us some of that terrific coffee and I'll write out the steps?"

"Good idea," I respond and stand to leave the room for the ground floor.

When I return, the flip chart he posted next to the window reads:

CHARACTER CULTURE ROADMAP

Step One – Vision for Culture. Senior leader commits to a vision for transforming to a Character Culture.

Step Two – Engage Workforce. Leaders and then entire workforce are enrolled in vision and process. Communication Plan created to keep everyone fully informed at every step. Consider creating an advisory team to support the transformation.

Step Three – Create a Benchmark. Assess the culture.

Sub-steps prior to formal assessment.

A. Poll staff on five questions:

1. What is unique and should be preserved at La Maison?

2. How do we best honour the finest of our history?
3. What would be required to make this organization even more successful?
4. How would leaders have to behave in order to achieve this level of success?
5. How would staff have to behave in order to achieve this level of success?

B. Summarize and categorize the answers

C. Customize the Character Culture Assessment as required

D. Administer the Assessment

E. Communicate Results

Step Four – Develop Goals and Plan to achieve Organizational Purpose.

Develop a plan to:

- Celebrate & leverage strengths
- Create systemic alignment
- Train and coach as required
- Establish milestones
- Measure progress

Step Five – Train and coach as required.

Step Six – Reassess and Refine.

- Measure & celebrate progress
- Refine plan to meet new goals

I place the tray on the nearest table and pour two cups. "Ok, I have more questions. What does 'Senior leader commits to a vision for transforming a Character Culture' mean exactly?"

"Good question. You are the senior leader. You have a vision for the culture. There are symptoms that all's not well. You're deciding whether or not to evaluate the health of La Maison." He takes the cup I offer and continues. "This approach takes the pulse of the business against a fundamental framework to determine if the direction is clear, the environment supports staff, and engages them to do their best work."

"That makes sense."

He moved to the table beside the window and tops up his china cup of black coffee. "As you're finding out, you can't succeed without the senior leaders reading from the same page. As Step Two says, it is important to include them quickly and engage them in everything that transpires."

"Gene, what if a senior leader can't buy into the plan? Either the direction or the way we do business?" I am troubled with the thought of conflict with the leaders. Leaders must be aligned and I suspect we aren't."

"Tough and significant issue. What would you do if you're the leader who can't buy in?"

I stand and look at the rows of La Maison anniversary pictures on the wall. Many of the staff have worked here a very long time.

"If I'd been with the organization for years I might just hang in to access my pension. I have heard this referred to as being a 'pension prisoner' and it appears commonplace. La Maison doesn't have pensions right now, but Nicolas and Connie are both long-timers. They know everything and everyone. Paul is the newest member and I want to be fair to him as well."

Gene joins me at the gallery of pictures. Charles smiles, front and centre, in every one. Thirty-four in total and no photograph for this year. Gene takes me by the shoulder, gently turns me back to him and looks me in the eye.

"It's your job, Claire, to ensure everyone has the opportunity to support this business. If they choose not to, then you'll have to make a tough decision. However, we aren't there yet, and hopefully won't be. The key is to involve everyone, early and fully, which is why we'll go through the steps in detail with the leaders on Friday."

"Thanks Gene, you're right. I am getting ahead of myself. Create Advisory Team to lead Culture Transformation. Please say more about that." We sit back down in the heavy, old chairs with the table between us.

"It has been my experience that if you create a small team, with a representative of each department, you will have the best opportunity for success. One person has to lead it, which in this case is likely you. Think about co-leading with someone from the staff who is respected and you trust. Also, include your three leaders on this team. The idea is authentic involvement, inclusive decision-making and deep understanding. Remember that there must be an ongoing and robust communication plan to support this project. That's essential."

"I love these ideas, 'authenticity, involvement, communication.' It will be so invigorating to see these concepts come to life in a meaningful way," I burst out excitedly, and make a few comments on my own note pad.

"Claire, communication is the lifeblood of any organization. The idea is to make sure that it's healthy and flowing abundantly to every single person. Speaking of communication, perhaps we should stop and you can take a look at the service agreement I drafted for your review," Gene suggests, taking a sheet of paper from his notebook.

The agreement seems reasonable especially since I had checked with Teesha regarding similar initiatives. I had certainly come to grips with the fact that I need help. If we accomplish these two objectives it will be worth much more than the cost, and will also be within the stipend left for this purpose.

"Gene, that's fine. May I amortize the cost over the life of the initiative?"

"Certainly Claire, and either of us can cancel the project with two weeks' notice. I'll ask you regularly for feedback on the service provided, and let you know how the project is progressing from my perspective. Ok, back to the conversation at hand. What's next?"

"Benchmark the current culture. How is that done exactly?" I continue.

"There are several steps here because you can't just hand people the Character Culture and say 'this is what we are aiming for.' Everyone needs to know what the value is to them. They need to understand that this isn't a 'nice to do' but is instrumental to the success of La Maison, and how La Maison's success links to their success. Everyone has to be part of the process and embrace it. So in saying that, there are several steps, as you see listed. The Advisory Team can lead this and I can definitely help facilitate, depending on what you decide," Gene says.

"So ultimately, every staff person completes the Character Culture Assessment; a customized version of the Framework which reflects our staff's answers to the five questions. Do the results show where La Maison stands and help us prioritize our efforts?" I ask.

"Yes. Step Four; Develop Goals and Plan to achieve Organizational Purpose, is a result of the assessment." Gene continues. "It's important to realize that all your 'people' systems such as recognition programs, performance appraisals, hiring systems, succession planning, and so on reflect your purpose and what you are trying to achieve, as well as your culture—how everyone works together to achieve your purpose."

"Looks logical. Step Five seems straightforward but a lot of work. Align human resource systems and provide training and coaching to support the plan. How long does all this take?" I question anxiously.

"Steps One through Four can be accomplished quite quickly, sometimes within three months. Step Five can take a while as you clarify performance expectations, train, coach, and make sure all your people systems align. Saying that, Step Five can take up to a year or even longer."

"Gene, as I told you, my only vision is survival. Is this more complicated than we need?" I ask.

"What is your alternative?"

"Everyone works harder," I respond, and realize that this takes me right back to the worry that hard work without focus, planning, and measurement rarely produces the desired result. "Never mind. I just answered my own question. Tell me more about the Framework. Why is it called 'Character Culture'?" I am truly curious.

"We are our character. In spite of our background, education, gender, and experience, we make choices every day that define us—choices which reveal who we really are. Building trust in leadership is critical to organizational success. Trust is a result of character and competence. Good character rests on the concept that every person is responsible for what they do, say, and achieve. Every person contributes to the success of La Maison. The Character Culture Framework summarizes what it takes to work with good character by defining both what's expected and how to work together to achieve it."

"Something tells me that not every organization would appreciate being that explicit." I shift in my seat. "Gene, you've offered a lot of information. Help me put the pieces together."

"My pleasure. The Character Culture Roadmap is a process for assessing and improving organizational culture which results in a higher level of trust and a more effective organization. The Character Culture Framework helps create clarity regarding 'what' you are trying to accomplish and 'how' to accomplish it."

Gene stands and draws four boxes horizontally on a clean piece of paper:

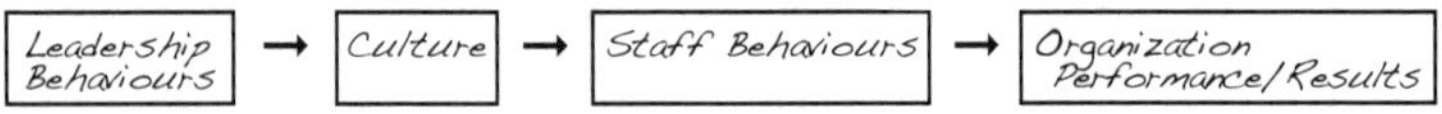

"To work backwards, the results aren't meeting target. That means the staff behaviour is the issue. That begs the question, 'what is the culture?' and that leaves you questioning leadership behaviour.

"If you employ the Character Culture Framework it would look like this," Gene explains.

"Ok, pennies are dropping. Thanks for helping me get clear. Gene, I want to introduce you and the work we are doing together on Friday. What's the best way to state it?"

"In your own words, Claire. What words would you use?"

"Gene, you truly encourage me to think things through for myself. Ok, something like this. La Maison is suffering. The key symptom is the financial stress, which is driven by guest reaction to the way things are working around here. I propose that we do what we know how to do—deliver great food and service as well as possible, while at the same time taking two steps. Establish a scorecard to project success and monitor results. Secondly, take the pulse of our organization which will help us understand where we're doing well and what we must improve. That is as simply as I can state it," I respond.

"Sounds like you're moving from Step One to Step Two—Enroll Senior Leaders. You know these people. What is the best way to enroll them?"

"Well, whatever I do, I mustn't threaten them. There's enough tension right now to cut the air with one of Nicolas' knives."

"What do you want to accomplish in the meeting?"

"I want to describe our situation in terms they relate to. I summarized the Profit and Loss Statements into a chart which clearly shows that sales have been sliding over the last few years, with the biggest dip in the last year. Costs have risen as well. Their help is imperative. This information will help inform the scorecard. At the same time, we start the process to take the pulse of La Maison in order to move in the right direction."

"Excellent summary. So what's your call to action? What help do you want from them?"

"I want them to understand the urgency of this initiative, schedule time with you to start working on the scorecard, and I'll ask for their help in forming the Advisory Team."

"Sounds like a start. How are you feeling at this point?"

"Better. I'm a concrete kind of person. Even though I don't understand everything entailed, I get that we are clarifying what we need to be successful, and taking a snapshot of where we are will help us determine what we need to fix."

"Good, one step at a time. See you Friday." Gene replies as he leaves my office.

Chapter Nine

Friday Managers' Meeting

Friday dawns with a cloudless sky—that magical time of year when trees are poised to attain full, magnificent splendour. The pond teems with life, and budding tulips surround the water.

The managers gather in the conference room. Everyone has the agenda in front of them.

All three look expectantly at me. The first agenda item is: Update on financial situation.

When everyone has settled with their beverage of choice, I begin.

"Thanks for being here so punctually. I know it's unusual to have a meeting on a Friday, one of our busiest days, but it's important to bring you up to date. The first agenda item will take a few minutes and then Gene LeBrun, whom you all know, will join us.

"Point one, we're in financial difficulty. This page illustrates the revenues and costs for the last five years," I state simply as I pass the document to each person. "Was anyone aware of this situation?"

"I knew revenues were decreasing and costs rising. We've been trying to manage it with smaller portions and cutting staff hours," says Paul.

"We haven't had that many complaints," adds Connie matter of factly.

I nod and continue. "As you know that begs a much bigger and longer discussion, as changing what we offer and how we offer it are serious decisions. However, the other urgent issue is that we're behind on our mortgage. We have to start paying our second mortgage immediately and repay arrears by the end of December. Is this news to anyone?"

The managers stay silent with eyes on agendas. As I suspected, they all knew.

"What can we do in the short term to deal with this?" I ask.

"Watch costs," all three answer immediately.

I nod again, knowing I must lead this in a different direction. I take a deep breath and plunge in. "Of course, that's my reaction as well, but rather than a sole focus, I want to update you on the thinking I have been doing with Gene, our resident Executive Coach. This is point two on our agenda. I've engaged him to help me sort out how to best be of service to the business and you. As you know, my background is in the area of leadership development which has been helpful in understanding our situation. This information is really important, so please stop me at any time if you have questions." I take a sip of coffee and organize my pages of notes before continuing.

"Here are my observations from the last few weeks. Many of our staff have been here a long time. I'm wondering how Charles' death has affected them? Has anyone asked them? And what are we doing in the short term about keeping them informed and engaged? In the longer term we need to think about a succession plan to deal with the turnover we'll inevitably face as people retire or want to work in a different way. And we, the leadership team, how clear are we on what we're trying to accomplish as well as how we work together?" I stop, take a breath and another sip of coffee.

"I resent the implication that staff has been neglected. I meet regularly with the front of the house team," blurts Connie, now beet red.

"Connie, no one is blaming anyone for anything. This seems like the obvious time to stop and take stock of where we are, where we need to go, and how we'll work together to get there."

"You made it sound like an insult," Connie persists.

"Certainly that was not my intention. My intention is to be open regarding what I've been thinking about and the issues that we, the leadership team, need to consider. Think about the metaphor of a two-sided coin. One side identifies 'what we want to accomplish' and the other side is 'how we accomplish it.' In other words clarifying our purpose and our culture." I state calmly.

Paul has been relatively quiet until now.

"I think you are making this more complicated than necessary. We continue on, do what has always worked, and watch costs. You're overreacting to this mortgage business." He looks me directly in the eye.

I remove my glasses and put them on the table.

"I have a responsibility to do what's right for this business and thereby what's right for all of us. If we continue the way we're going, there may not be a business by the New Year. What I ask is your support in clarifying our goals and ensuring that we all behave in ways that support them. This may seem high-handed of me. You've all worked here for years and things were going relatively well until my uncle fell ill. We have reached a significant moment in time. My greatest hope is that we can work together, doing the right things, to ensure success for all."

"What exactly are you proposing and what's the cost?" Paul asks.

"I propose two things. We create a scorecard that projects what we must achieve and we track progress diligently. Secondly, we conduct a health check-up on La Maison by using an organizational assessment," I respond as I pass out the two-page document.

"Let me give you a few minutes to read this. The assessment is based on this document which describes what is called a

Character Culture. I'll ask Gene to join us in a few minutes to talk about creating the scorecard and describe this aspired culture in detail," I explain as I stand to go and find Gene. I am aware of the click of my high heels on the wide-slatted wooden floor as the room is so quiet.

The three managers look at each other in silence.

"This doesn't feel right to me. This is going to give her too much information and let her intrude in our areas," Connie states indignantly.

"I want to know more about this before commenting," shares Nicolas.

"How much is this really going to cost? Gene; scorecards; assessments; meetings. And she wants extra money every month for the mortgagee too?" Paul shakes his head.

"I'm making a list of our questions. What should we ask?" says Nicolas picking up his mechanical pencil and turning over the agenda.

"I want to know what she's really up to. She obviously feels she can just come in here and change everything Charles has done. She thinks she's above us because she had a big leadership job. I don't trust her for a moment. No matter what happens, she gets this house, so she has nothing to lose," sputters Connie.

"Connie, we all know the building is mortgaged to the hilt. Charles was struggling to keep everyone employed and it cost a fortune. There's no equity in the house and I doubt there's much in the business. How do you know what she thinks anyway?" Nicolas asks.

"I can tell by the look on her face. I've always been able to read people." Connie retorts.

"How do you know you're right?" Nicolas asks.

"I just know. They try and tell me otherwise but they're just lying to make themselves look good. And by the way, why are you being so mean to me?" Connie continues.

Nicolas shrugs and shakes his head. *He's been in this labyrinth with Connie many times. This is precisely why her staff just tolerates her. They know that truth and facts are irrelevant. Connie believes what she chooses to believe and repeats her "insights" to anyone who will listen. Over the years most people have learned to keep her at arm's length. Charles knew what was going on but felt she was dedicated to the business so he turned a blind eye. He also knew that whenever he called her to task, she would call in sick, which affected the day-to-day operation.*

"Ok, back to the issue at hand. Let's read this document before Gene gets here. We know he's a good guy and Charles believed in him," Nicolas reasons.

"I don't know. I just know I don't trust her," Connie repeats.

All three managers read the document while waiting for Claire and Gene.

Chapter Ten

Leaders Review the Character Culture Framework

I return with Gene, who sits beside me at the round table. I smooth my skirt and pour a glass of water.

"Tell us again what you're trying to do with this exercise?" Paul asks before I have a chance to speak.

"Let me pass the baton to Gene who's going to take us through the scorecard concept as well as the Character Culture Framework," I announce.

Gene mimes taking the baton and smiles at the group. "Thanks Claire. We're proposing a two-step process. First of all, that I lead you, and perhaps the supervisors who report to you, through an exercise to develop a scorecard. The purpose is to track, on one page, your key goals or key performance indicators and results. This tool will help put La Maison on the road to sustainability. The second step is to coach an initiative to assess your culture, which includes: clarifying your purpose; where you are headed, the impact of that direction, of which the scorecard is part; and your values—how you work together, all set against an effective Framework. We identify gaps and create a plan to bridge any gaps so La Maison can be sustainably successful," he explains.

"What do you imagine this initiative, if that's the right word, will look like?" Nicolas asks.

"Good question and yes, I think the term 'initiative' is a good one. There's more information to add, but for right now, let's start with the principle. You must decide if these are worthy activities. If yes, then let's establish a date to work on the scorecard, and in terms of the assessment, a good approach is to create an advisory team to lead the project. First, what questions do you have about a Character Culture?"

"I think a scorecard sounds like more paperwork and the Framework looks idealistic. Who actually works that way?" Paul states.

"Here's what we know for sure. Think about Scotty Bowman. He holds the record for most wins as head coach in National Hockey League history—nine Stanley Cups with three teams: in Montréal with the Canadiens, in Pittsburgh with the Penguins, and in Chicago with the Red Wings. Then he added four more as Head Office Executive with Pittsburgh, Detroit, and Chicago. That's a total of thirteen Stanley Cups. Do you think that every person on the team knew how to win a game? Of course they did. Do you think that every player knew the score at every second in the game? That level of clarity is critical for success. Secondly, do you think that every player knew the role they were expected to play?" Gene asks.

Every head is nodding.

"So the job of leadership is to clarify what's expected of every person in the organization and to coach everyone to success. Look at the five Pillars in the Framework: Create Clarity, Commit to Accountability, Coach for Performance, Cultivate Collegiality, and Collaborate for Results. Isn't that what you expect of your workplace? It's certainly what the research tells us engages people. And, as you will see, we will ask your staff their point of view, which will either validate this approach or help us customize it," Gene adds, taking a moment to look at each of the managers at the table.

* X-Ref to Gilbert Model

"What questions do you have before I tell you about the second part, the Character Values?" Gene pauses.

"It just seems over specific, too petty to me. Where does individuality come into it?" Connie complains.

"Great question, Connie. Let's continue the comparison to a hockey team. Whose job is it to recognize and encourage the strengths of each player?" Gene asks.

"I guess it's the coach," Connie responds.

Nicolas leans forward in his seat. "It's absolutely the job of the coach. Players have positions which correspond to their strengths. Ultimately, they win when they learn to work together for the benefit of the team."

Gene nodded his agreement. "Nicolas is absolutely right. One of the first tenets of employee engagement is to know what's expected at work. And Nicolas' point leads us right into the Character Values. In Canada, we have people from every part of the world living and working here. Everyone grew up in their own value system, including people born in Canada. Establishing what's expected in this business helps people understand how to play on the team to make this workplace successful for their own benefit, as well as that of everyone else. Respect, compassion, courage, and integrity. I know I aspire to work that way, as do my clients. Don't you want those behaviours from Claire and everyone else you work with?"

"How can we argue with that? But for my part, I'm interested in how we get there," Nicolas states.

"First, does everyone agree with moving forward?" Gene asks.

Again, the managers nod.

I think it's time to contribute to the discussion. "Let's schedule our scorecard meeting. Then we can discuss who will be on the Advisory Team, in addition to you as the senior leaders. Hopefully we can include a representative or two from each of the functional areas. We let the staff know what we're doing and why we're doing it."

Paul looks up, startled. "Claire, you aren't suggesting that we tell them we're behind in the mortgage payments, are you?"

"Yes, I'm recommending that we tell the staff the truth and ask them to be part of the solution. They have a vested interest in this organization. Why wouldn't we tell them?" I ask, keeping my tone even. It's irritating to think that one group is not as trustworthy as another because of their job title.

Paul rises slightly out of his chair. "What if they tell our customers or competitors that we're in trouble?"

"We'll ask them not to and explain why not. We need to be consistent in what we, the leadership team, are saying and how we say it." I want to make sure everyone is communicating consistently and accurately.

Connie, who is now leaning forward as well, quickly interjects. "This does seem to be an unusual approach."

"I believe that the staff, like you, the leaders, have a right to know the truth. If we don't trust people to be supportive and appropriate, then why are they working here?" I continue.

"Your uncle believed in protecting people," Connie counters.

"Well, do you want to know the truth?" I ask, putting my glasses back on as I sit back in my chair.

"Not really, but apparently I'm forced to. I'm a manager." Connie continues with a sarcastic tone.

I can't resist the next question. "Does that mean you are more intelligent, more committed or more trustworthy than the staff?"

Connie's eyes harden. She sits even straighter in her chair and stares directly ahead.

"What I'm asking is that we create a team to assess the state of our business. If the assessment determines that all is well;

good. If we have improvements to make, we'll work together to make them. And I promise that we will do this in a way we can afford and that you'll be part of every step. Do I have your agreement?" Claire asks.

Reluctantly, each person nods.

The managers spend the next twenty minutes creating an employee list from the various departments to approach them to participate in what Gene calls the Culture Advisory Success Team, or CAST for short. George Paige, the long time and well respected head bartender who is also known for his sense of humour, will be asked to co-lead the team with Claire.

Paul and Connie leave.

Nicolas stays behind and approaches Claire. "I know this can't be easy," he starts. "Your uncle was good to me and I've enjoyed the chance to work in such an excellent kitchen. I appreciate the opportunity to be creative and lead others. I'll help you any way I can. May I book some time tomorrow? I would really like to clarify a couple of points," he asks. We book a meeting after lunch and he heads back downstairs.

Chapter Eleven

Confronting Leaders' Concerns

Nicolas and Connie arrive in my office mid-afternoon. Connie asked to join us as well. I know they don't have much time to spare so we chat briefly about the lunch hour, which was busy, thankfully, and start our meeting.

"What's on your mind?" I ask.

Nicolas scrubs the lunch hour stains on his white jacket with his apron as he asks, "We both want to talk a little bit more about what we're doing. This is definitely more complicated than when Charles ran the business. We used to focus on good food and service; nothing more than menus and costs were ever discussed."

I appreciate the comment. It feels honest. "This must indeed seem odd and time-consuming. Everything I've read and experienced tells me that we need a good, concrete, clear plan for both what we're trying to achieve and how we go about achieving it. What do you think is the downside of this path?"

Connie responds. "We aren't saying it's a bad idea Claire, it's just that it's new to us and we're all worried about the time involved and what might come out of it."

"What might come out of it?" I ask, thinking that the power of Gene's open-ended questions has rubbed off on me.

Connie continues. "Well, if the staff is so fully involved, the leaders worry that they might not be necessary, for one thing."

"What else are they worried about?" I let the use of "they" continue, as Connie typically avoids speaking directly for herself.

Language is so important, but this isn't the fish I want to fry right now.

Nicolas jumps in with more honesty. "That we'll be micromanaged. Charles gave us a job and let us go about it. All this clarity might be another word for losing control."

"I'm so glad you're telling me this. I didn't realize you were thinking this way. What's the best way to deal with these fears?" I move from the round table by the window to my desk to get my notebook. I want to jot down these priority issues.

"What's the bottom line? What do you hope will happen out of all this?" Connie asks as I sit back down again.

"Incredibly important question. My most fervent hope is we continue to employ the same people, that everyone knows exactly what we're trying to accomplish, that we'll know how we're expected to behave, and that the business is amazingly successful. I can't predict exactly what'll come out of this, but I commit to do everything in my power to ensure everyone has a chance to flourish at La Maison. I know you're being asked to proceed on faith and that's quite a request."

Nicolas is up next and has stopped working those stains. "I get that you want to track our progress but why are we talking about culture? What do you really want the advisory team to achieve?"

"Chef, that's a big question. First of all, we'll ask the employees what matters most to them. We'll include their perspective in the assessment. Then we create a plan to work together as effectively as possible. I have worked in organizations that were frustrating and discouraging where people wanted to work hard and feel proud, but the culture robbed them of their enthusiasm. We also know from the research that the majority of Canadian employees are less than fully engaged. We know what truly engages is a clear sense of purpose, of mastery in their craft, and autonomy. Nicolas, that's the opposite of micromanagement. It is about creating clarity so everyone can confidently make the right decisions by supporting one purpose and acting on our agreed upon values."

Connie continues and she looks very upset. "What if we find that we have some problems with our culture? Won't that be an embarrassment for us?"

I'm actually pleased with the candid question. "We'll have to face the truth. And that can be hard, especially if employees haven't had an opportunity to offer their point of view in a long time. This will be a challenging process but just like you want to be involved, so does our staff. We know that engaged people are more energized, innovative, and productive. We can only turn this business around if everyone is on board and doing everything possible to reach our goals. Perhaps that's already the case, but let's find out."

Nicolas' turn to comment. "So the biggest downside is that we might not like hearing there are improvements to be made, and that we, the leadership team, are responsible for the problems."

I think we are really getting to the heart of the matter. "Imagine if every organization had the courage to face the truth and put energy into making improvements, rather than assigning blame? We're also opening the door to innovation and that's exciting. It seems to me that this process should be ongoing and widespread. How else can we keep getting better? You know the old chestnut, 'if you aren't moving forward, you're falling behind.'"

Connie is still looking uncertain and her cheeks are flushed. She's tapping the table as she says, "Claire, this is new to us. We had a job. We worked hard. Things stayed more or less the same. I'm not to blame for what happened here."

"Connie, I hear things are different for you and that this change is difficult. We have to take full, informed control of what's going on and do what it takes to improve the business. I promise to include you and the leaders every step of the way. And we'll ask leaders to include the staff. What gives me hope is the restaurant's been successful for a long time. We have the same core group of employees and we still have, as you well know, many regular guests.“

"Well, it looks like you're committed to this path," Nicolas sighs, looking me straight in the eye.

"What choice do we have? If we don't figure this out together, it's possible there won't be a restaurant come the New Year."

The silence is heavy as the three of us look out the window at the new life on the water and well groomed grounds. I can't help but wonder if I'll be here next spring.

"Ok, what's next?" asks Nicolas, as Connie nods ever so slightly.

"Thank you. You have no idea how important your support is. How do I reassure Paul in case he has the same issues?"

"You need to have the same conversation with him," Connie replies matter-of-factly, as Nicolas and I nod agreement.

Before the supper hour, the four of us sat down in the conference room. Paul's fears mirrored those of Connie and Nicolas, although they were stated more aggressively.

We also crafted a letter to the staff which explained what we were doing, and why we're doing it, with the promise to fully update them weekly in their team meetings.

Chapter Twelve

Chartering the Culture Advisory Success Team (CAST)

Gene met with the senior leaders and supervisors to create a scorecard. He and Claire agreed this was an urgent step in order to establish goals and track progress. Gene explained that a sustainable business has three legs: economic, people, and environmental viability. Together, they determined that for La Maison, economic viability means projecting and tracking revenues and costs between now and the end of the year. People viability includes customer satisfaction, employee productivity, turnover, and innovation. Environmental viability includes reducing costs through energy conservation, recycling, and contribution to local community. They were able to establish metrics to track results on a weekly basis. Every supervisor believed that the goals were achievable and knew how to track results.

The first Culture Advisory Success Team meeting was facilitated by Claire and George. Gene spent an hour coaching an enthusiastic George on his role. He and Claire rehearsed how to charter a team. There were eight people representing every aspect of the business: full-time and part-time servers, kitchen staff, hostesses, and bus people, as well as the three senior leaders. The supervisors were encouraged to sit in on the meetings in addition to being updated by their own leader. After much explanation, inclusive facilitation, and discussion, the charter—an agreement on how to work together, was developed.

Culture Assessment Initiative—Culture Advisory Success Team (CAST) Charter

- **Purpose of CAST:** To lead an initiative to assess the current culture of La Maison du Parc, determine and prioritize steps towards aspired culture, and create a roadmap to achieve the aspired culture in order to maximize revenue, profit and organizational potential.

- **Project Outcomes:**
  A Benchmark of current culture which includes our purpose (within two months)
  B Detailed roadmap to achieve our aspired purpose and culture (by end of third month)
  C Monitor execution of the roadmap; and
  D Re-evaluation of our culture in one year

- **Measurement:** A brief report (two pages maximum) and a plan that all staff understand and can implement (as determined) at the end of Project Outcome B.

- **Timelines:** Benchmark culture within two months, roadmap by end of three months, reassessment in one year.

- **Our Ground rules:**
  - Claire and George are leading the initiative. We are all responsible to each other regarding commitments, and if we can't meet a commitment/meeting we contact one of them prior to the commitment/meeting.
  - Have fun.
  - Listen openly.

- Build on ideas.
- All technology off during meetings.
- Any issue that is presented as confidential is not discussed beyond the CAST team.

- **Progress.** How do we acknowledge progress? Develop a CAST Workplan, with timelines. Claire and George keep it updated with our input. Report progress at the beginning of meetings.

- **Barriers.** What do we do if we are off track? Acknowledge immediately as a group and update the CAST Workplan to get us on track.

- **Accountability.** Who holds us accountable? We hold ourselves and each other accountable. Claire and George are ultimately accountable to make sure commitments are kept.

- **CAST Meetings and Membership.** How we work together: Meet as the CAST every other week for one hour. Meet in small groups as required. Create a budget for this project and update the budget monthly. Remain as a team for one year. Evaluate our team at the end of every three months.

- **Communication with Staff**
  At the end of each CAST meeting we create one consistent update message for other staff (if anyone asks us what is happening). Leaders update their staff during their weekly team meetings. An area of the bulletin board will be used to communicate information regarding the initiative. The updated CAST Workplan will be posted bi-weekly by George.

The CAST crafted their first communication to the rest of staff. The memo, which everyone received a copy of, stated: *"We have formed a team (CAST—which stands for Culture Advisory Success Team) to explore our current culture and determine what our culture should be in order to support the success of La Maison. We have all been grieving Charles' death and want to do everything in our power, in his memory, to ensure that we are maintaining and strengthening the high standard of food and service our guests deserve. You will be involved in the initiative at every step. Your own leader is your primary source of information. Feel free to discuss this initiative with any member of the CAST. You are also welcome to attend our meetings as a guest. Just let your leader know. Thank you for your support and hard work."*

Chapter Thirteen

CAST Explores the Character Culture Framework

The CAST assembled for their first action meeting. Gene facilitated the session and requested myself and the three leaders to join the meeting thirty minutes after the start. He explained that having us present might cause hesitation with some of the staff in answering questions candidly. He also asked that we remain open to any comment or feedback, as this type of information can be helpful.

"Here is the first question. George is going to note what you say on a flip chart. What is unique and should be preserved here at La Maison?" Gene asked the group. Answers popped up quickly and George captured the responses on the flip chart.

"The house and the view are beautiful."

"We have a reputation for good food."

"Many guests knew Charles and ask about him."

"Most of the staff have been here a long time. In the old days we were very well treated."

"Really helpful answers; thank you," Gene said when the group became quiet. "George is going to post the flip chart so you can add to it if another idea comes to mind. Next question—how do we honour the best of our history?"

"What if we let our guests know what is happening at La Maison? They ask us and we don't know what to say," shared one of the long term servers.

"Good idea. George and I will gather information for the time being."

"I would like to see something that memorializes Charles," suggested a bus person.

"What if we have something on our menu that Charles really liked and name it for him?" offered a sous chef.

"All good thoughts. We will capture what you have said for now, and feel free to add to the list. Just ask George." Gene explained. "Here is the next question—what's frustrating about working here?"

"Leaders give contradictory directions."

"The cliques."

"We don't really know what's going on with the business, and it makes us wonder if we should be looking for other jobs."

"The lazy people aren't dealt with, and it's discouraging."

"Politics take up too much time."

"There's a lot of gossip and conflict, which is uncomfortable."

"Leaders don't really listen to us. There are lots of things we could say that would help the business, but they don't really want to hear."

"There's tension between the back of the house and front of the house."

Gene took notes and acknowledged each speaker. "Thank you for the honesty. This is exactly the kind of behaviour we want to change. Your job on the CAST, is to encourage people to work together in a positive manner, to articulate functional, constructive behaviour. I'm now going to invite the leaders into the room."

As we entered, Gene explained that we were fortunate to have some good answers to the first three questions. The leaders were reading the flip chart as they sat down.

I look around the big table. Today, as usual, I dressed in business mode: a blue blazer, white blouse, and tailored grey pants, accented with my grandmother's pearls and matching earrings. I want to convey that this is business. The restaurant, the people here, are important.

"Thank you. Your work is critical, and I'll tell you why. The document I'm passing to you is a summary of the Profit and Loss Statement for the last five years. This inverted hockey stick means that our revenues have been decreasing steadily the last few years, and have really slid in recent months. The second graph indicates that costs have been rising. We can't continue in this pattern. To this end the leaders have created our first scorecard. We did this quickly in order to establish goals and track progress. This form of goal-setting and tracking progress is an element of the initiative and will be updated with your input in the future.

"Further, how we work together is critical to our success. Most of the places I have worked, and I imagine you as well, were described as 'dysfunctional.' I experienced many of the behaviours listed on the flip chart. My most sincere hope is that we have a higher purpose than just running a good business, which is terrific, but I'm totally committed to developing a truly functional and successful organization where everyone is honest, caring, and enjoyable to work with and wants only the best for everyone else. I see our 'higher purpose' as creating a business where each person who interacts with us, whether as a guest, an employee, a supplier, and the greater community, is treated respectfully, fairly, honestly and honourably. It is also important to work with high integrity suppliers who provide safe, quality food, and in turn, deal with us fairly."

Paul stands at this point. He rolls his eyes at my words and heads down the stairs with a shake of his head.

Everyone looks startled and immediately turn to me for my reaction. I grit my teeth and sit back down and say quietly, "I'll follow up with Paul after we adjourn."

Gene stands and continues.

"We have two more questions to ask you. George has agreed to continue noting your answers on the flip chart. Thanks George," Gene remarks as George takes his place to the right of the new sheet, marker in hand.

"First question—What would be required to make this organization even more successful? Before you reply, take a couple of minutes and confer with your neighbours in groups of two or three. One person please jot down your answers."

At first there was silence and then everyone started to talk at once. After ten minutes Gene asked for one idea per group until every idea was listed. Within five minutes George had filled two pages of flip chart paper.

WHAT WE NEED:

- *To know what we are aiming for and how we are progressing*
- *To have leaders listen to us when we're telling them what guests are saying*
- *To be more in the know about all aspects of the business*
- *To feel like we're valued by our leaders for what we know and do*
- *Some kind of formal feedback system. We had performance appraisals once but they were badly handled and we gave up on them*
- *To believe that everyone wants the business to be successful rather than "just doing their job"*
- *To trust our leaders to tell the truth*

- *To trust that our leaders say the same thing to our face as they say elsewhere*
- *To have collaboration with all the departments*
- *To be more strategic about our offerings*

Gene took the floor again as George put up more paper. "Thank you. This is of great value. Let me ask you the second question. Answer in your small groups first, as before, please."

(5) "Now two lists. How would leaders have to behave in order to support successful business, apart from what you have just said? And how would staff have to behave?" This time there was no pause. Ten minutes later the list looked like this:

LEADERS:

- *Everyone needs to treat everyone else respectfully*
- *Leaders must recognize good performance and confront poor performance*
- *There needs to be encouragement and reward for bringing ideas forward*
- *We should know what's going on in the whole restaurant, all the time*
- *It should be fun to work here*
- *Each person should know what decisions can be made without having to ask a supervisor*
- *It has to be clear how everything works—raises, promotions, what basis we hire on*

STAFF:

- *We can ask questions about anything and get an honest answer*
- *There is an overall sense of fair play*

- *We do more for the community like giving away left-over food*
- *We talk more to staff and guests we don't know that well*
- *We tell the leaders when something needs improving (and suggest the improvement)*

Gene takes the floor once more. "Thank you again. These are entirely reasonable thoughts. They also align to a concept that we want to show you now. We want to present a well researched model of the requirements for a functional, high trust, effective workplace. It is called a Character Culture Framework because it has evolved out of the Character Community Movement of York Region, to the north and east of us. Claire and George, will you please pass out the document? Thank you. I think you'll be surprised how similar your insights are compared to what you'll read on these pages."

Gene continues once everyone has had a moment to look over the document. "In a Character Culture everyone is treated with respect and in turn is expected to act respectfully, with integrity, courage, and compassion. I will talk more about these values in a few moments but we should start by talking about how to be sure that La Maison is successful.

"In order to support organizational success, five Pillars have been developed. The first Pillar is, Create Clarity which means as Claire said, that you ensure there is a vision, a purpose for La Maison and everyone knows it and supports it. Just like in a hockey game, everyone knows both how to score and what the score is at all times. This is why the leaders created the first scorecard, to get everyone in the game.

The second Pillar, Commit to Accountability, means that there are positive consequences for doing the right thing, and consequences for leaders and staff who do not support the purpose and values."

At his words the CAST started applauding.

"What are you clapping for exactly?" Gene asks.

"For years the people who didn't care about their work, and did their jobs poorly, were not dealt with at all. It has brought all of us down," stated one of the long-time servers.

"Thank you for the comment. Candour is appreciated. How many of you feel this way?" Gene asks.

Almost every hand in the room rises including Nicolas. Connie, a dark scowl on her face, is the lone exception. Gene writes in his notebook and continues. "Ok, this is exactly the kind of issue we're working on. Clarifying who is accountable for what, and what that means. The leaders have done the best they were capable of and are now open to other approaches. For now let's move on to the third Pillar, Coach for Performance. This means that every person helps every other person to be successful and provides information to help the business flourish."

Another hand goes up. "Gene, does that mean I can give my boss feedback?" asks a bus staff.

"Not only *can* you, but in a Character Culture you have a responsibility to support his or her success. Of course there is a time, place, and way to communicate your perspective," Gene answers.

"I think I'm liking this Character Culture idea," is the reply.

Gene smiles and moves on. "Pillar four, Cultivate Collegiality, means that people trust each other, feel they belong, and are a valued member of La Maison. The atmosphere is one where people feel safe and engaged in their work and organization. Dr. Dave Williams, an astronaut, medical doctor, and renowned leader calls this 'positive energy.' The point is, it's healthier to work in a positive environment than a negative one.

"The final Pillar is Collaborate for Results. You touched on this at the beginning of the meeting. Have a simple process for encouraging and harvesting ideas that will make the restaurant better, in big and small ways. This also ensures that the leaders are doing what is right for La Maison, rather than just their own department.

"Why don't we take a break and give you time to read this in detail? We can answer your questions when you're ready," Gene suggests.

When everyone has finished reading Gene asks, "First of all, does the Framework include all the ideas you generated earlier? That's imperative. George, perhaps you would note this information on the flip chart?"

George pulls out a purple marker and prepares to write on a fresh piece of paper.

"We decided that everything is covered and much more. It really spells out what my group has been trying to convey," responds a server.

"Thank you, you are 'validating' the model. Anyone else? It's essential that your point of view is properly captured."

"No, we're good. My partner and I went through point by point and it's covered," answers a bus staff.

"Alright, but we can go back to this. We'll go through the same exercise with the entire staff before we finalize the next step. What other questions do you have?" Gene asks.

"It seems like everyone has a hand in making the business successful, beyond just doing our own job. Is that the intention?" asks a server.

"Yes, that's an astute observation and it's definitely the intention. If you work here, you contribute to the welfare of the organization beyond your specific role," Gene affirmed looking at everyone in the room.

"So that means every person is responsible for the success of this business?" questions Connie.

"It means much more than that. It means that we're all responsible for what we say and do. And yes, everyone is expected to do their part to support their colleagues and the business," Gene responds.

"I thought leaders are responsible for the business?" Connie asks.

Gene replies with, "The leaders are key, without question. However, every person and every action determines the success or failure of an organization. Guests don't care about your position, they care about their experience. Every person who has ever worked, is currently working, or will ever work at La Maison du Parc has either helped or damaged the business. How everyone acts with each other, the guests, the community and suppliers also counts. Who believes this to be true?"

I put up both hands and eventually everyone in the room, after looking at each other, raise their hands.

"Good, that's a really key point. Other questions?" Gene requests.

"There is nothing here about customer service or food, for heaven's sake," says one of the kitchen staff.

"You're absolutely correct. The Framework is generic. We must, as we continue together, define the two or three values that are unique and important to La Maison. The work we'll all do on the 'purpose' will help us," I attest.

"Does this mean that you really want everyone to be honest with everyone else, no matter their role? Even part-time people?" asks one of the serving staff.

"You just said that together we're stronger. The key is to agree on how and when to offer our perspective, as Gene said earlier," I add.

"Are you saying that we could tell all our leaders how they come across? Really?" asks a server.

"Yes. Also as Gene has commented, we're all here to help each other and thereby, La Maison, be more successful." I answer.

"What do you think your uncle would think of this?" Connie asks me.

"I think Charles was ahead of his time. He had a vision for a restaurant that would offer elegant dining to everyone and provide a good living for the staff. In my heart I know he'd want us to adapt to new circumstances. La Maison is his legacy and we must do what we believe will ensure her longevity," is my honest response.

"I don't know how to do many of the things on this list. I also suspect that the leaders don't know either. Are we expected to just do it somehow?" asked another server.

"What a great question. We know we'll have a lot of work to clarify what each one of us must do to truly make this a Character Culture. I commit that training and coaching will be available so we can learn and apply the skills. We'll also incorporate the concepts into all of our Human Resource systems such as how we hire, orient, train, offer feedback, and evaluate performance. That's a pivotal part of the journey," I emphasize.

"What do you think La Maison would be like if everyone behaved this way?" Gene asked as he held up the two pages.

"I think it would be an incredibly focused and rewarding place to work," George offered as he took a seat at the table. "Honestly, I believe we can do it. Come on guys, we're decent and hard-working people! This doesn't seem so odd, just very explicit and new to us as we have never put anything like this in words before."

"Well, the first step is to evaluate where we stand right now. We would like your thoughts on whether or not George and I take all the teams through this same exercise and summarize the answers. Then this team compares the answers to the Character Culture Framework. The question on the table is, should we do an assessment based on this Framework, which can then be customized if there is anything unique to us? All staff participates. The results will help prioritize our plan. Comments?" Gene waits patiently.

"So what you are saying is that there's an assessment based on the Framework which we can tailor to La Maison… sort of a special order. Then the whole staff completes the assessment. What will that tell us exactly?" George asks.

"The report that's generated from the assessment will tell us what's working and what needs to be improved. You, the CAST, will help create a plan to leverage our strengths and improve where required," Gene responds.

Nicolas jumps in at this point, "I think we'll learn what we need to focus on. I'm also clearer on why the flip side of the coin is important. It sounds like if we work together in these very specific ways we'll rally all our resources to make this a restaurant that benefits not only the guests, but everyone involved," he adds enthusiastically.

"So," Gene directs, "put up your hand if you think we should move forward. This means going through this exercise with staff, compiling their answers, comparing their responses to the Framework, customizing the assessment if need be, asking the staff to complete the Character Culture Assessment, and creating a plan/roadmap from the report," Gene listed on his fingers.

Every hand in the room, except one, immediately shoots up. Everyone looked at Connie. With a frown she too raises her hand.

Chapter Fourteen

Showdown with Paul

Paul texted me during the meeting. "Come to my office asap."

I descend to the ground floor to stretch after sitting, to see what's happening in the restaurant and follow up with Paul. I'm irritated by both the fact that he left the meeting in the way he did and to send a summons in this way. There better be a real emergency to explain this. I know that the situation is volatile, but I'm not sure how to deal with it other than just include him in everything that's going on and be totally honest with him. And, thinking about my lawyer buddy Hal's refrain, document everything that appears critical.

Paul is on the phone and hangs up as soon as I enter his office. I notice that there are no pictures or anything personal in sight.

"What is it Paul? I feel like I've been summoned," I say bluntly.

"You have been summoned. You are a naïve and idealistic woman. You're going to tank this business. Honour? Who the hell are you kidding? Suppliers, customers, and staff will rip us off every chance they get. My job is to protect this business. There is only one side of the coin. Make money. Either you let me run this business or I'm out of here. Don't think I won't do it."

I'm stunned by his aggressive tone and can't formulate an immediate reply.

He stands and pokes his finger at me as he talks.

"I know how to run a business. Successful people don't make decisions based on 'honour.' Success is having the biggest bank account, driving the car you want, getting the best deal. I tolerated that social responsibility-community nonsense on the score-card, but this is the last straw. You may give money away to charity, but only when you can afford it. Success is about freedom and power. I'm disgusted that Charles left you this business. I predict you'll be closed within the year."

"Let me tell you what I think," I reply slowly but firmly, buying as much time as possible to organize my thoughts and get my racing heart to a normal rate.

"I doubt you can say anything that'll change my opinion," Paul retorts.

"First of all, I can't imagine what it's like to be in your position. Your experience gives you a certain skill set. Secondly you believed that you'd have total control of this business. Finally you find my beliefs and values contradictory to yours. This must be a truly frustrating and difficult time for you," I respond, knowing that this level of acknowledgement is the only hope to have a decent conversation.

Paul just glares at me with steel in his eyes.

"What did Charles tell you when he hired you?" I ask.

A pause ensues which I'm determined not to break. It's critical that I wrestle control of this conversation.

Finally, he talks.

"He knew he was dying a year ago. He wanted someone to steer the ship as he backed away. Of course I gave the usual rhetoric about engaging people and all that crap. It doesn't take much to figure out the flavour of the month. Both of us knew that the restaurant needed someone who understood costs and could make sure no one was stealing."

"Paul, you must know that the concept of capitalism has evolved past a 'profit first and only' model. Organizations can't pretend they have no impact on society, the economy, and the environment. We have responsibilities as employers and business leaders. Are you telling me that you disagree with this perspective?"

"When you put it that way, I have no choice. This is ridiculous. No notice, I'm leaving right now."

"Thanks for letting me know Paul. Please put your decision in writing," I calmly request, while strongly suspecting that there will be no letter. It's unfortunate that Charles chose someone so unlike himself in Paul, but so be it. Somehow I feel deeply relieved as I return upstairs to document the conversation and its results. Good thing that I have been learning the financial side of the business; I'm going to need it. In my heart I know that this was inevitable and ultimately it will be good for La Maison and all of us.

Chapter Fifteen

Results of the Character Culture Assessment

Paul's disappearance did not create much stir. Laura was his only direct report and I spoke directly with her as well as the other leaders. The only explanation was Paul had chosen to leave La Maison and we were grateful for his contributions and wished him every success. We posted this information in a notice that included me taking over his duties, with Laura's help.

The restaurant buzzed in preparations for the summer season which officially started the third weekend in May, Victoria Day weekend. The protected herb and flower gardens were showing definite promise as Gene and George visited the team meetings, asked their five questions without the team leader in attendance, explained the Character Culture Framework, and compiled the responses for the CAST to review. The CAST made the decision to conduct the assessment in its original form, as key issues are covered. They decided to develop La Maison specific values as a follow-up action.

Everyone was excited the day the assessment began. The CAST continued to communicate the purpose of the exercise and what would happen to the results. A question box and Twitter page had been set up to answer any queries about the process and outcomes.

A couple of anonymous questions targeted candour and confidentiality. What would be the backlash if they answered in a truly honest manner? The CAST reinforced that all input was appreciated, and confidential... the more honest, the better. If anyone sensed that they were experiencing repercussions as a result of the assessment, they were to take their case to the CAST.

Finally, two weeks later, with one reminder, the assessment was complete.

The CAST convened on a Tuesday when La Maison was closed. The contracted maintenance staff was doing a thorough clean of all equipment, including stoves and hoods. They were also setting up the wrought iron patio furniture and installing the massive outdoor barbeque.

We met at a local private club to review the results and develop a plan. Charles had been a long-time member of the old club resting on the shores of Lake Ontario. We promised to host their staff Christmas party in reciprocation. Gene helped facilitate the meeting. The agenda sat at the front of the large room with the huge windows, overlooking the lake.

The Meeting Agenda:

- Review the results of the Character Culture Organizational Survey/Report
- Plan next steps:
  - Determine priorities regarding the five Pillars plus Employee Engagement Score
    - Develop a draft plan to tackle short term and long term actions
  - Determine priorities regarding the four Character Values
    - Develop a draft plan to tackle short term and long term actions
  - Develop a draft plan to develop/attach behaviours to the Organizational Values
  - Develop a process to include all staff in the planning stage and finalization of the plan

Gene stood to review the results. "This slide reveals that 'Cultivate Collegiality' is your highest score. 'Create Clarity' is the lowest score. Several questions support each of the Pillars. Let's drill down and take a look at the five highest responses."

Character Culture Pillars — summarized results:

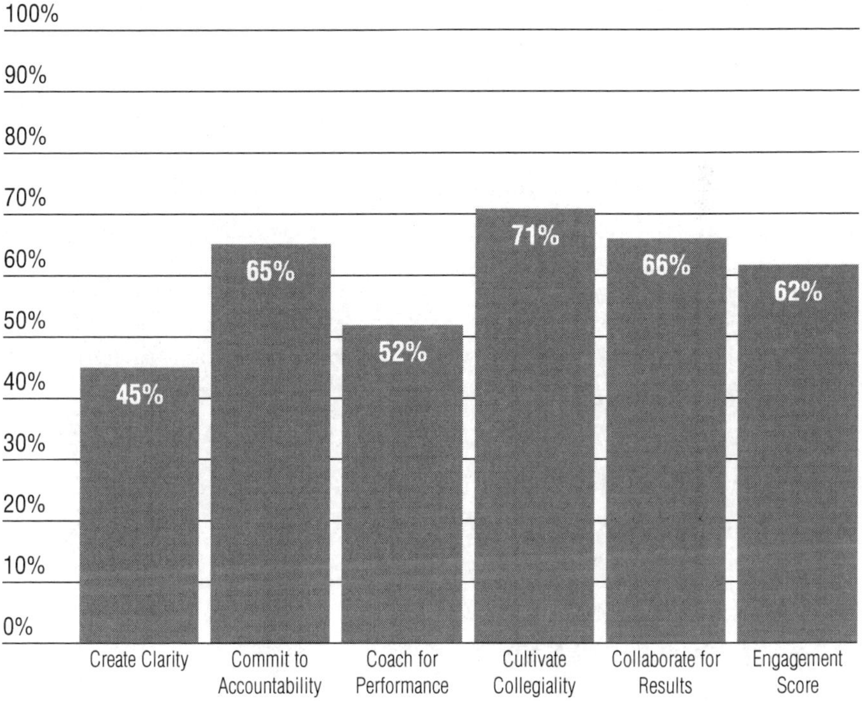

The five highest Character Pillar individual answers:

- Colleagues support each other (Cultivate Collegiality)
- Commitment to the success of the business (Commit to Accountability)
- People know each other (Cultivate Collegiality)
- People care about each other (Cultivate Collegiality)
- Enjoy the physical plant (Engagement)

"This is important. We must leverage strengths in the plan," Gene emphasizes. He shows the next slide with the five lowest answers.

The five lowest Character Pillar individual answers:
- Ability to speak up regarding issues that can help individuals/organization (Coach for Performance)
- Understand the purpose of the business (Create Clarity)
- Clarity re organizational progress (Create Clarity)
- People being held accountable (Commit to Accountability)
- Feedback on opportunities for improvement (Coach for Performance)

After a few comments regarding the information, Gene and I broke the team into small groups and provided a template to create the short and longer term plan. We circulated among the groups, coached and encouraged the team members. The groups were debriefed, the CAST reach agreement and the first part of the plan was drafted.

Draft One Year Plan to Achieve our Purpose and create a Character Culture

Short Term—over the next two months

1. The CAST develops a compelling purpose for La Maison:
    - Strategies:
        - Conduct a focus group with current, past, and potential guests.
        - Create an "Innovative Idea" form and box for staff members to contribute ideas on how to improve the business. The CAST reviews and publishes feedback on each idea.
        - Servers ask guests what they value about La Maison and what can be done to make the restaurant even more appealing.

- Once the compelling purpose has been created and tested on staff, Organizational Values will be collaboratively created to support the purpose, e.g. Offer Warm, Respectful, Outstanding Guest Care, Leverage La Maison's Charm in Every Way, and Offer Interesting and Healthy Food

2. The leadership team clarifies roles and responsibilities given the new team member (Claire). Publish the structure and information to all staff and stakeholders. Claire continues to learn all aspects of the business. As she works through the positions, she updates the training materials for each job. The end result is an updated training program for each position.

3. Each leader meets with every member of his/her team to clarify job expectations and align the individual job to the purpose of La Maison du Parc.

4. The CAST refines the scorecard which determines qualitative measurement in the three categories: Economic, People, and Environment. The Character Framework will be embedded in the scorecard as appropriate and aligned to the three legs of the sustainability model.

5. Every Monday morning, results will be posted on the bulletin board, emailed, and posted on La Maison's private Facebook page for staff.

6. There will be a monthly All Staff Meeting to review results, celebrate progress, and communicate opportunities, barriers, and solutions.

7. Leaders meet with their team as a group once a week to identify team goals and progress.

8. Leaders meet monthly with each staff member to identify individual goals, update progress, determine new goals, as well as create ongoing opportunities for innovation, learning, and development. The team member is expected to offer feedback to the leaders as well; what is valued and what could create additional value.

✶ *Longer Term*

A Training programs will be offered to leaders and staff in order to support the Character Culture Pillars, Character Values and the two or three Organizational Values of La Maison du Parc.

B Claire works with the CAST to align the Human Resource systems to support the purpose and culture.

C The Character Culture Assessment is scheduled for one year in the future to benchmark progress.

Gene walked to the front of the conference room and shows the next three slides.

Character Values — Results from the Survey

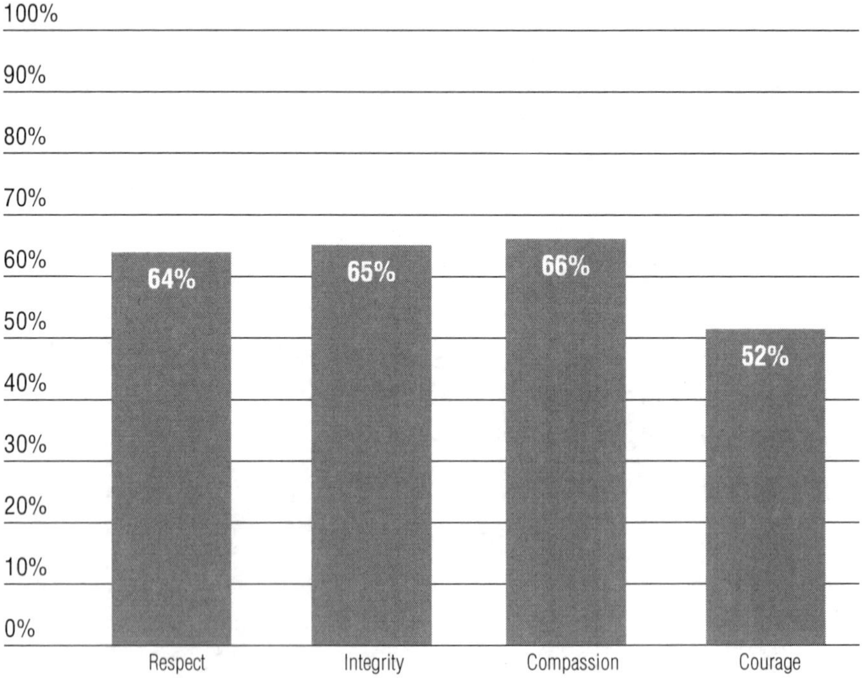

The five highest Character Values individual answers:

- People are considerate and kind (Compassion)
- People speak positively about the organization (Respect)
- People practice good etiquette by saying hello, good-bye, please and thank you (Respect)
- People keep promises and commitments (Integrity)
- People are always assessing how to do things better and more effectively (Courage)

The five lowest Character Values individual answers:

- People listen actively when I am speaking (Compassion)
- People involve me in decisions that affect me (Respect)
- People make assumptions about motives, thoughts, and feelings (Integrity)
- I say "yes" when the answer is yes and "no" when the answer is no (Courage)
- People describe their own experiences as a way of providing support (Compassion)

We continued working together in the same fashion and are pleased to create the final part of the plan.

Draft One Year Plan Resulting from Assessment/Report for Everyone to Practice the Character Values

Short term—over the Next Two Months

1. Leaders will review the Character Values in their weekly meetings. One Character Value per meeting. The objective is to clarify what is meant by each Value, solicit La Maison examples, and explore ways to continue to apply the behaviours.
2. Everyone will read the booklet, *Communicating in a Character Culture; with Tact, Integrity, and Courage.* Everyone offers one piece of positive feedback per week. Developmental feedback is mutually exchanged by leaders and direct reports in their one-to-one meetings.

Longer Term Plan

A Claire and the CAST research training programs to support the following skills:

- a Active Communication—Speaking from your "I" and active listening
- b Courageous Conversations
- c Emotional Intelligence Training for Working in a Character Culture
- d Coaching for Performance (for leaders)

Their first All Staff Meeting is scheduled two weeks later. Leaders commit to distribute the Draft One Year Plan to all staff and ask for feedback. The input will be reviewed and incorporated by the CAST. Any idea not incorporated will be explained by leaders at team meetings. The final One Year Plan will be distributed prior to the next All Staff Meeting.

The group thoroughly enjoyed working in different surroundings, as well as the hospitality offered by the Club. The momentum and feeling of accomplishment was profound.

Chapter Sixteen

All Staff Meeting

It's the third Tuesday in August. La Maison is closed on Tuesdays so we can consistently open Monday. Our long holiday weekends are precious and La Maison is doing solid business. I'm thrilled to see the whole staff together in the main dining room. Gene has joined us for this celebratory meeting. Every person in this room received a copy of the final One Year Plan last week after all questions were answered in team meetings. We're all here, overflowing into the sun room, an intimate room to one side of the main dining room. When everyone quieted down, I opened the meeting.

"Thank you for being here today. I know it's your day off and if you're full time, please schedule another free day. Part-time people, we'll make sure you're paid. We have much to celebrate and a little bit of work to do, so let's get started. When Charles passed in February, it was a difficult time for you. The leaders, as well as myself, are so grateful that you kept La Maison running. He'd be very proud of you, as am I.

"I want to assure you that La Maison will absolutely stay open until the end of the year. Your efforts have already resulted in increased revenue and a slight decrease in costs. I'm very confident that the plan resulting from the assessment, which everyone has reviewed and had an opportunity to comment on, will guarantee our future well past the end of the year. We've much to be grateful for.

"So, to back up a little bit, since I arrived in March it's been an intriguing and exciting journey. We formed the Culture Advisory Success Team, affectionately known as the CAST, assessed our culture, and created short term and long term plans, with your help, to target the right course. This is to ensure success for everyone here and a long life for La Maison. I'm committed to stay and work with all of you. Our dream is to create a truly functional, effective business where every person who interacts with us, whether a guest, staff member, supplier, or community member feels respectfully and honestly treated. We want you to utilize your individual strengths, generate innovative ideas, and be an engaged, energized, enthusiastic member of our team who looks forward to coming to work.

"Having said all that, what are your questions at this point?"

One of our servers speaks up. "Are you saying that we might not be open past December 31st?"

"I'm totally confident if we work together and stay on the plan which you have co-created, we'll be celebrating in this room January 3rd of next year. Further, once we're on target we'll explore other ways for La Maison to flourish even more magnificently. When she flourishes, so will you. That's my promise."

Nicolas eagerly invites George and the CAST to pass their trays. Connie is smiling and chatting with people around her, which is encouraging.

George and the team offer flutes of ice wine and crystal glasses filled with our alcohol-free house sangria garnished with mango slices. Everyone stands for the toast.

"From the bottom of my heart and on behalf of Uncle Charles, as well as everyone who has worked so hard to arrive at this significant moment—thank you. We can't do this without you. And a special nod to our coach, Gene, who stood by us for the last few months. I'm delighted you are here. Let's celebrate this meaningful day with a lovely meal prepared by Chef Nicolas and our kitchen brigade. First let's drink a toast to Charles and our future."

The excitement and energy in the room is invigorating. As people raised their glasses, we unveiled a portrait of Charles with the small plaque inscribed with his original mission statement. **La Maison du Parc is a place where local people can dine on well prepared, good quality food at reasonable prices, in a beautiful setting, all while being respectfully and well attended.**

"This portrait will be hung in the foyer with a view of the pond and the park. You inspired this idea. Thank you."

Smiles and tears accompanied the quiet words, "To Charles."

Chapter Seventeen

Gene and Claire's Final Conversation

Gene and I are back in my office where this journey began. It's the end of September. The restaurant is at capacity every day. The patio is fully reserved and the bus staff is able to clean and prepare a table within three minutes to accommodate the line-up. The scorecard is posted weekly and everyone is aware of our progress. I'm beginning to relax and enjoy my new life. I even enjoy an early coffee most mornings on the bench by the pond.

Gene and I met every other week for the first little while and now we meet monthly. He has helped me stay on track and I'm very grateful for his help. Our discussions have focused on supporting the leadership team. We now include the supervisors in our weekly meetings. Gene attended three meetings and coached the leaders on how to deal with any staff having trouble with the new, inclusive, communicative, innovative workplace.

We're sitting at the small round table overlooking the grounds. Little row boats dot the pond and our benches are constantly occupied with people enjoying the day and the view.

"Claire, your initial goal was financial sustainability by the new year. What is it like watching that scorecard meet or beat your projections?" Gene asks knowingly.

"We're definitely on track Gene, as everyone knows by the scorecard. We're paying off the arrears so I'm very grateful for that part. Thank you for your help. I also want to let you know that Lou was here for lunch this week. We're now on good terms."

"Good news. What do you see as the next area of focus for you?"

"I keep thinking about your description of communication as our lifeblood. Nicolas and Connie are doing their best but need help. The staff is talking to each other more but it still feels awkward. I think we need to do some work around honest feedback, both giving and receiving, to make sure that everyone has all the tools and techniques needed to make ourselves and La Maison all we can be. This is especially important as there are several new restaurants opening up in the neighbourhood, so we are facing more competition."

"You're right, communication is the place to start, competition or no competition. Why don't we set a new agreement to focus on developing the skills in that particular area? Does that seem like the right next step?"

"Absolutely. And perhaps we could think about creating a learning module that everyone can access? That would be very powerful."

"When do you want to start?" Gene asks.

"Tomorrow. Why wait? To use your metaphor, communication is the lifeblood of the organization and it must be healthy. Let's make that lifeblood flow as richly, positively, and abundantly as we can." Gene smiles as we turn and soak in the beautiful, flower-filled view and the satisfaction that comes from progress. This evening, Teesha, Hal, Ping and I will celebrate at our little bistro. I know they are thrilled for me. I'm thrilled for the team at La Maison who's worked so hard, and my uncle, for providing this unexpected and extraordinary opportunity.

Part Two

The Evidence:
The Character Culture Framework

The Character Culture Framework has grown out of the collective experience of thousands of practitioners in their roles as leaders, researchers, consultants, and coaches—doing the real work of establishing and sustaining a character culture in diverse organizational contexts. It has also been influenced by lessons learned in my over thirty years of professional practice and by the findings of experts and thought leaders across many fields who have in common, the pursuit of healthy behaviour and healthy organizational cultures.

Finally it's important to note that the Character Culture Framework will continue to be fine-tuned to reflect lessons learned from organizations striving to make a Character Culture their reality and also take into account the findings of ever-evolving research.

Making Connections with Part One

In Part One of *Building a Character Culture,* you read about Claire Gilbert's first steps in transforming the organizational culture of La Maison du Parc, a restaurant she unexpectedly inherited from her uncle.

In this Part Two, you will learn about the Character Culture Framework, including the context and rationale for its development and research foundations organized as follows:

Using the Lessons of Leadership and Coaching — in Practice and in Research

What is Character and Why is It Important?

Where there is agreement about character, both in research and in practice, it's evident that everyone has character and that character is what determines how we live our lives. Abraham Lincoln has famously said, "Reputation is the shadow. Character is the tree."

Webster's English Dictionary defines character as, "the complex of mental and ethical traits marking a person, group or nation."[1]

> "Character is the whole person, everything we believe, say and do, in our own unique way."
> —*Leadership by Engagement*

In another definition character is said to be, "A composite of good moral qualities typical of moral excellence and firmness blended with resolution, self-discipline, high ethics, force and judgment."[2]

Our character, therefore, is much more than what we try to display for others to see. It is who we are even when no one is watching. Character is the map that guides our intentions, our thoughts, our feelings, and our actions.

"Character is higher than intellect. A great soul will be strong to live as well as think."
—Ralph Waldo Emerson

While there is no consensus on a definition of character, the Character Culture is founded on four Character Values: respect, integrity, compassion, and courage. It is useful however, to consider this view of character in the context of current research.

The work of Petersen and Seligman stands out as seminal in providing a thorough and active definition of character. In their landmark handbook, *Character Strengths and Virtues,* these renowned researchers draw on their survey of diverse world cultures to develop a systematic classification and measurement of widely valued positive traits. They approach good character in terms of separate strengths—from curiosity and integrity, to kindness, fairness, humility, and hopefulness—each of which they say exists in degrees.

"Character fundamentally shapes how we engage the world around us, what we notice, what we reinforce, who we engage in conversation, what we value, what we choose to act on."[5]
—Gerard Seijts, Jeffrey Gandz, Mary Crossan, and Mark Reno

This ground-breaking research continues to influence researchers and practitioners across sectors, as they not only struggle with defining character, but also with how character can be assessed. For example, Jeffrey Gandz, Mary Crossan, Gerard Seijts, and Mark Reno of the IVEY Business School at Western University, draw on the failures of leadership and identify leadership character as a central theme. Their findings led them

"Leadership in these complex and turbulent times requires an amalgam of competencies, character, and commitment. We, of course, know a great deal about competencies—90 percent of leadership development over the past few decades has focused on competencies and skills. But what is emerging as increasingly important is the emphasis on leadership character and encouraging people to use their values."[6]
—Jeffrey Gandz

"Trust is one's willingness to be vulnerable to another based on the confidence that the other is benevolent, honest, open, reliable, and competent.

Benevolence: unfailing goodwill, empathy and caring, offering encouragement, expressing appreciation, being fair and responsive

Honesty: telling the truth, integrity, self-awareness, authenticity, accepting responsibility

Openness: open communication, sharing important information, sharing power, delegation, shared decision-making

Reliability: keeping promises, honouring agreements, being consistent, predictability, diligence, dedication

Competence: inspiring a shared vision, co-creating possibilities, striving for results, problem solving, conflict resolution, elevating energy"[9]

—From *Trust Matters* by Megan Tschannen-Moran (2004)

to the following conclusion: "Business leaders who focus on the long-term performance of their organizations must demonstrate ten virtues plus an overriding or 'über-virtue.'"[3] The ten virtues are humility, integrity, collaboration, justice, courage, temperance, accountability, humanity, transcendence, and drive. The über-virtue is judgement, and the authors concluded that it "allows leaders to balance and integrate these virtues in ways that serve the needs of multiple stakeholders in and outside their organizations."[4]

Stephen Covey stands out among educators as one who has deepened our understanding of character. In his landmark book, *Seven Habits of Highly Effective People*, Covey coined the term "character ethic" to encompass attributes such as integrity, humility, courage, patience, and the Golden Rule—"Do unto others as you would have others do unto you." In his view, "Eventually, if there is no integrity, the challenges of life will reveal one's true character."

Character matters; about this there is no debate. As Dov Seidman points out, "virtually everyone from consumers and customers to judges and juries have now begun to view organizations from a 'characterological' viewpoint."[7] What he means by this is that they are paying more attention to, and care more about, the "inner life and character" of those with whom they do business. They have begun to ask themselves whether the organization has integrity. Does it have a character?

"As much as it sounds like a homily, science has shown that caring and honest behaviours increase trustworthiness."[10]

—Dov Seidman

Character then is foundational to the organizational culture envisioned in this book. Gene and Claire know that healthy behaviour is an "inside-out" activity. It is the character of each member of the staff that will create the success of La Maison du Parc. Leadership character is the key to reaching the high level of employee engagement and commitment that is characteristic of high performing workplaces. In short, "character is the core." *Leadership by Engagement.*

> "I look for three things in people. The first is personal integrity, the second is intelligence, and the third is high energy level. But if you don't have the first, the second two don't matter."[13]
> —Warren Buffet

Bringing Trust into the Conversation: Is Character Enough?

It is widely understood that trust lies at the centre of our challenges and opportunities. Many researchers refer to trust as the glue that binds organizational participants to one another as well as the lubricant that contributes to greater efficiency when people can have confidence in other people's words and actions (Covey; Lencioni; Tschannen-Moran). Preeminent business leader, Warren Buffet, is known to have said to his employees, "Trust is like the air we breathe. When it is present, nobody really notices. But when it is absent, everybody notices." Everyone at La Maison is paying attention to Claire and the leadership team. Are they trustworthy?

> "Trust makes us feel safe. It allows us to function and thrive in an uncertain world ... Trust for instance, allows us to rely on each other, to divide up labour, and form teams knowing that each will do his or her part and to share confidences with others."[14]
> —Dov Seidman

If trust matters to this extent, will having good character be enough to generate and sustain trust, trust that makes it possible to create what we care most about in our organizations?

A definition of trust sheds light on this question. Although trust is difficult to define because of its complexity, Tschannen-Moran's survey of definitions of trust across many fields led her to this definition: "Trust is one's willingness to be vulnerable to another based on the confidence that the other is benevolent, honest, open, reliable, and competent."[8] In short, of good character.

In another definition from Stephen Covey, trust means confidence. In his view, when we trust people, it means that we have confidence in them—"in their integrity and in their abilities."

Character + Competence = Trust

What is noteworthy in these arguments about the importance of character in the context of the whole person is the way in which the qualities of integrity, truthfulness, and candour are embedded. Also of significance is the reference to competence as an essential dimension of trust. What might be inferred is that character on its own does not equal trust. Instead it is both character *and* competence that are needed to bring about and sustain high levels of trust.

> "Trust is a function of both character (which includes integrity) and competence."[15]
> —Stephen M.R. Covey

Covey clarifies this. He argues that most of us tend to think of trust in terms of character—of being a good or sincere person or of having ethics or integrity. And although he acknowledges that character is foundational and essential to trust, he stresses that character alone is not enough. Trust, he maintains, is a function of two things: character plus competence.

Gandz et al agree that competence matters. Competencies, they contend, define what a person is capable of doing. In the assessments of leaders these researchers undertook, they looked for intellect as well as organizational, business, people, and strategic competencies. They also identified commitment as critical as it, "reflects the extent to which individuals aspire to the hard work of leadership, how engaged they are in the role, and how prepared they are to make the sacrifices necessary to succeed."[11]

In the end, however, Gandz et al support the assertion that "above all, character counts." It counts, they say, because, "it determines how leaders perceive and analyze the contexts in which they operate. Character determines how they use the competencies they have. It shapes the decisions they make, and how these decisions are implemented and evaluated."[12]

Can shining a brighter light on character—which is what the Character Culture Framework does—be justified? The response is a categorical, "Yes!"

Support for this claim can be found in research conducted by Jim Collins. In the good-to-great companies he and his research team identified, greater weight was placed on character attributes of employees than on specific educational background, practical skills, specialized knowledge or work experience. It was not that specific knowledge or skills were unimportant, but these traits were viewed as being more teachable—or at least learnable—whereas other dimensions such as character, work ethic, dedication to fulfilling commitments, and values were viewed as being more ingrained.

Even so, according to Covey, competence must be viewed as essential in organizations that have as their goal achieving high trust, as it is the differentiating and often ignored side of trust. In a character culture, it may appear that the emphasis is exclusively focused on character. After all, it is a "Character" Culture Framework, not a "character-competence" culture framework. The opposite is the case. Close examination of the Framework, provided in sections that follow, will illustrate that the competence needed to make wise choices, and decisions that impact the culture of the organization, is embedded as necessary and indispensable in a character culture. Competence behaviours then are enacted in concert with the character behaviours in the Character Culture Framework. Claire must not only behave with integrity, she must also learn and show expertise about the restaurant business as quickly as possible in order to be seen as a trustworthy leader.

The Interplay of Beliefs and Values

Values are at the heart of any organizational culture, and beliefs held by those in the organization influence how the values are expressed in decisions and behaviours. This is the complexity of the belief-value connection. According to Senge, beliefs are, "consciously held, cognitive views about truth and reality. They are the theories people hold—how they explain their world."

> "Values are beliefs that people have about what is important or worthwhile to them. Values influence behaviour because people seek more of what they value. If they can get more net value by behaving in certain ways, they will. Values therefore can be seen as the guideposts for behaviour."[16]
> —Mary Crossan, Jeffrey Gandz, and Gerard Seijts

Senge explains that these deep beliefs and assumptions can change as experience changes. In his view, we live in a world of self-generating beliefs which remain largely untested. We adopt those beliefs because they are based on conclusions, that are inferred from what we observe, plus our past experience.

And so for Senge, beliefs drive values and in turn, our behaviours. This, he says, is because "our ability to achieve the results we truly desire can be eroded by our feelings that:

- Our beliefs are *the* truth
- The truth is obvious
- Our beliefs are based on real data
- The data we select are the real data."

> "Values are your guidelines regarding how to treat yourself, your organization, and others."
> —*Leadership by Engagement*, 2008

Likewise, Kegan and Lahey draw attention to the intricacy of the beliefs and values relationship. For them, the beliefs and values connection is grounded in a psychological dynamic they refer to as a "competing commitment." What this means is that alongside our visible and expressed values is a rival set of values of which we are unaware.

> "Both beliefs and values are invisible to the naked eye and rest within the inner world of those who hold them. They become visible through our actions and behaviours."[17]
> —Patrick Lencioni

The beliefs-values connection presents an enormous challenge for organizations intent on creating a culture of engagement and commitment to organizational purpose. Not only must they be aware of what is visible to the naked eye—the behaviours that can be observed—but they must also take into account what lies beneath the surface—the competing values that are tied to beliefs and assumptions that have not surfaced.

This is why there is an emphasis in this book, and future books in La Maison du Parc series, on a coaching approach. The coach approach of asking about intention, thoughts and feelings helps individuals understand their own underlying beliefs and assumptions rather than dictating specific behaviour.

The Complex Interrelatedness of Beliefs, Values, and Culture

The Character Culture Framework sets out a vision for organizations that is founded on core Character Values, or convictions that everyone in the organization holds about how they must behave to fulfill the organization's mission and purpose. As such, it is important to consider how beliefs, values, and culture are interconnected and mutually reinforcing.

> "Organizational culture is more like an ecosystem, a highly sophisticated, interdependent cosmos of evolving organisms with a profusion of interrelationships. More simply defined, culture is the way things *really* work, the way decisions are *really* made, emails *really* composed, promotions *really* earned and meted out, and people *really* treated every day. And it matters. Culture is a company's unique character, its lifeblood; it lives in each company's achievements."[20]
> —Dov Seidman

Wide-ranging research confirms that culture is a powerful force shaping work enjoyment, work relationships, and work processes and productivity. That culture is made up of the values, beliefs, and behaviours shared by a group of people, is a given. But what is the relationship among beliefs, values, or culture?

The following sampling of definitions illustrates in part the dynamic and reciprocal interaction between beliefs, values, and culture.

- Culture is made up of the shared assumptions, values, and beliefs that show people what is appropriate and inappropriate behaviour. (Chatman & Eunyoung)
- Culture exerts a powerful influence on values formation—behaviour in one culture could be prohibited in another. The content of values is largely culturally determined and culturally sensitive. (Seidman).
- Culture "refers to the norms of behaviour and shared values among a group of people. Norms of behaviour are common or pervasive ways of acting that are found in a group, and that persist because group members tend to behave in ways that teach these practices to new members, rewarding those who fit in and sanctioning those who do not."[18] (Kotter)

Edgar Schein, whose studies of organizational culture are among the most notable, cautions that organizations, just like individuals, have their own personalities, and this uniqueness means that while there may be similar beliefs and values in organizations, no two cultures are alike.

The reason this is so can be explained in Schein's definition of culture. For Schein "culture is a pattern of shared basic assumptions that a group has learned as it solved its problems of external adaptation and internal integration. This has worked well enough to be considered valid and therefore, to be taught to new members as the correct way to perceive, think, and feel in relation to those problems."[19]

In thinking about organizational culture, it is useful to keep in mind the three interrelated levels that Schein contends are at play:

1. basic, underlying assumptions that encompass our unconscious, taken-for-granted beliefs and values that determine behaviour, perception, thought, and feeling
2. espoused beliefs and values that include our principles, goals and aspirations, and may or may not align with our behaviour or artifacts
3. artifacts which are the visible and tangible elements of culture, including observed behaviour that may be hard to interpret.

Over the past three decades, the subject of organizational culture has captured the attention of both scholars and business leaders as they examined what it is high-performing organizations do to bring about and sustain success. Peters and Waterman, in their best-selling book *In Search of Excellence,* were among the first to identify successful companies and then shed light on the strategies that led to their results. They argued that a company's success could be attributed to an organizational culture that was decisive, customer-oriented, empowering, and people-oriented.

It was, in fact, Peters and Waterman who were among the first to draw attention to, and make popular, the concept of "organizational culture." At the time, organizational culture not only entered the lexicon of the business literature as a catchphrase, but also became the focus of others in their search for deeper understandings about culture which would offer a blueprint for culture that, if emulated or at least adapted, might lead organizations to success.

Why Organizational Culture Matters

This leads to the question, "How important is culture to the success of an organization?" There is consensus in the business literature that an organization's best opportunity to thrive lies in the mastery of culture (Collins, Covey, Seidman). This assertion is not lost on discerning and astute leaders.

> "A company's culture is essentially the organization's soul, shaped through success and setback."[21]
> —Patrick Lencioni

In addition, a wide range of empirical research has resulted in well established links between organizational culture and organizational performance. Bain and Company research (Rogers, Meehan, & Tanner) asked business leaders from around the world to assess their usage of, and satisfaction with, particular management tools, such as mission and value statements, strategic planning, and mergers and acquisitions.

Their survey results confirmed that management issues such as corporate culture, environmental protection, and knowledge management have now moved to the forefront as priority. Results also showed nearly seventy percent of these executives agree that "culture provides the greatest source of competitive advantage." In fact, more than eighty percent of those surveyed believe that "an organization that lacks a high-performance culture is doomed to mediocrity."

> "Mastery of culture is no longer a job for just those at the top of the organizational chart. An organizational culture represents the collective action of all the individuals that comprise it, so on the journey to make the most of the new conditions of today, it is incumbent on everyone who wants to do well to understand the intricacies of how culture works."[22]
> —Dov Seidman

This research also found that in "standout" companies, the picture looks different. These companies inspire loyalty from employees who want to stay and be part of a team. They generate commitment to go the extra distance, to do the right thing, rather than just the easy thing. At these companies, people not only know *what* they should do, they know *why* they should do it.

How do these companies ensure that everyone acts in the best interests of the company when no one is watching? The answer, these researchers assert, is "culture."

In fact, it has been debated that organizations with a rare and hard-to-imitate culture enjoy a competitive advantage. This comes as no surprise to leaders of successful businesses who are quick to attribute their company's success to their organization's culture.

Culture is powerful for three primary reasons:

1. Individuals are selected and indoctrinated so well.
2. Culture exerts itself through the actions of hundreds or thousands of people.
3. All of this happens without much conscious intent, and this is difficult to challenge or even discuss.

This research indicates that, from developing strong and productive cultures, organizations may derive many benefits, all of which promote consistency, encourage coordination and control, shape employee behaviour, and enable the organization to be more efficient and successful. These benefits include improved alignment of the company towards achieving its vision, mission and goals, high employee motivation and loyalty, and increased team cohesiveness among various departments and divisions.

It was Peters and Waterman who debated that the stronger the culture and the more it is directed toward its overarching purpose, the less there is need for policy manuals, organization charts, or detailed procedures and rules. In the excellent companies they identified, "people way down the line know what they are supposed to do in most situations because the handful of guiding values is crystal clear."[25]

"Worldwide business leaders identified corporate culture to be as important as corporate strategy for business success."[23]
—Paul Rogers, Paul Meehan, and Scott Tanner

On the heels of this focus on organizational culture by Peters and Waterman, came the influential research of Jim Collins and his associates. In *Built to Last: Successful Habits of Visionary Companies*, Collins and Porras reported on their six-year research project which asked, "What makes the truly exceptional, enduringly great companies different from the comparison companies, and what were their common practices?"

"Without exception, the dominance and coherence of culture proved to be an essential quality of the excellent companies."[24]
—Thomas Peters and Robert Waterman (1982)

They confirmed the power of culture in "enduring great companies." Subsequent works by Collins which include *Good to Great*, and *Great by Choice*, co-authored with Morten Hansen, further reinforce and substantiate claims not only about "core ideology" but also about the culture that emerges.

Understanding the Character Culture Framework

In the previous sections, it is argued that creating and sustaining strong and positive organizational cultures can mean the difference between a successful and high-performing company or not. In the sections which follow, the Character Culture Framework is presented as a model whose features hold promise for bringing about healthy organizational cultures.

"Inner work life is the mostly invisible part of each individual's experience—the thoughts, feelings and drives triggered by the events of the workday."[26]
—Teresa Amabile and Steven Kramer

A Character Culture as Fundamental to Organizational Health

Organizational culture that has character at its core is essential to organizational health. Support for this claim can be found in the research of Lencioni, who equates organizational health with integrity. He contends that an organization is healthy when it is "whole, consistent, and complete, that is, when its management, operations strategy, and culture fit together and make sense." This is why the five Pillars are at the bottom of the graphic. Start with *what* you are trying to achieve, *why* it is significant, the *impact* it will have and then *how* people behave to create the whole.

Although Lencioni's definition of a healthy organization seems to be more expansive—for example, he states that organizational health is more than culture—the Character Culture presented here has all the ingredients Lencioni claims are needed to bring about and sustain organizational health.

> "As inner work life goes, so goes the company."[27]
> —Teresa Amabile and Steven Kramer

Support for this assertion can be found in the work of Teresa Amabile and Steven Kramer, that they describe in *The Progress Principle: Using Small Wins to Ignite Joy, Engagement, and Creativity at Work*. Drawing on their landmark study of "inner work life," these researchers reveal how organizations can have both high levels of employee engagement and success.

They found that the secret lies in creating the environment for great inner work life—the conditions that foster positive emotions, strong internal motivation, and favourable perceptions of colleagues and the work itself. They confirm that observable actions in an organization merely form the tip of the iceberg—which might be referred to as the "culture" iceberg. "Inner work life", they state, "is the enormous bulk that is hidden beneath the water's surface."

> "Great inner work life is about the *work*, not the accoutrements. It starts with giving people something meaningful to accomplish … it requires giving clear goals, autonomy, help and resources —what people need to make real progress in their daily work. And it depends on showing respect for ideas and the people who create them."[28]
> —Teresa Amabile and Steven Kramer

One of the goals of the Character Culture is in fact to foster the kind of inner work life that Amabile and Kramer describe.

> "At a time when enterprises can stretch around the globe, culture is the glue that holds a complex organization together. It inspires loyalty in employees and makes them want to be part of a team. It motivates people to do the right thing, not just the easy thing. At companies with winning cultures, people not only know *what* they should do, they know *why* they should do it."[29]
> —Paul Rogers, Paul Meehan, and Scott Tanner

A Character Culture in its unique and Character- Value-based approach can create the conditions to bring about positive inner work life. It also holds the best promise for addressing the challenges of engagement that organizations around the world now confront.

To support this claim, consider the types of organizational cultures identified by Chatman and Eunyoung Cha. These researchers began their study with the premise that cultures can be distinguished by values reinforced within organizations. While they found there is no single type of organizational culture, and that organizational cultures vary widely from one organization to the next, commonalities do exist. They proposed that organizational cultures, within and across industries, can be characterized by seven dimensions:

1. Cultures that are flexible, adaptable, and innovative, and are characterized by a flat hierarchy. Positional roles and other status distinctions tend to be downplayed.
2. Stable cultures are predictable, rule-oriented, and bureaucratic, and prevent quick action. As a result, they may not be adaptable to a changing and dynamic environment.
3. People-oriented cultures value fairness, supportiveness, and respect individual rights. There is a greater emphasis placed on, and expectation of, treating people with respect and civility.
4. Outcome-oriented cultures emphasize achievement, results, and action as important values.
5. Detail-oriented cultures are characterized as emphasizing precision and a focus on minutiae.

6. Team-oriented cultures are collaborative, collegial, and promote cooperation among employees. Cross-training is fostered to increase capacity to help one another when needed.
7. Aggressive cultures value competitiveness and outperforming rivals. They often fall short of social responsibility.

> "'Hard' approaches to management are those seeking to influence behaviour by pressuring people to do things they would not have freely chosen. 'Soft' ones are those seeking to influence behaviour by nurturing people to build commitment to doing a good job."[30]
> —Steven Kelman and Sounman Hong

This typology of cultures provides a useful reference point for an initial categorizing of the Character Culture. Although there is no one-of-a-kind found in this classification of cultures, a mix of several could hold true of a Character Culture. These include innovation, people-orientation, results-focus and teamwork.

A more promising depiction of the nature of a Character Culture can be found in the research of Kelman and Hong, who examined the links between "hard," "soft," and "tough love" cultures, and organizational performance. Their findings show the importance of a culture mixing "hard" and "soft" features—one that can be described as "tough love," in improving performance. "Strong presence of the two hardest cultural features—accountability and direction—improves performance when paired with a warm climate."[31]

Yet another classification of cultures that provides a useful reference point for understanding the Character Culture Framework is Adam Grant's hypothesis about a hidden dimension of corporate culture—giving and taking. "Giver" cultures as Grant describes them promote an approach aligned with the Character Culture; that is, "helping others, sharing knowledge, offering mentoring, and

> "Organizations have a strong interest in fostering giving behaviour. A willingness to help others achieve their goals lies at the heart of effective collaboration, innovation, quality improvement and service excellence. In workplaces where such behaviour becomes the norm the benefits multiply quickly."[32]
> —Adam Grant

making connections without expecting anything in return." This is in stark contrast with the "taker" cultures Grant describes in which "the norm is to get as much as possible from others while contributing less in return."

A cautionary note here—although the Character Culture Framework has essential Character Values and unique guiding principles, it's important to recognize that all organizations have what Rogers, Meehan, and Tanner refer to as "unique personality and soul." They argue further that it is a combination of two key elements that comprise "winning cultures": high performance values and behaviours, and a distinctive personality.

It is important for La Maison to develop its own unique organizational values in addition to the Character Culture Values. This step was part of the plan developed by the CAST as a result of the Character Culture Assessment.

Organization of the Character Culture Framework

The Character Culture Framework provides a unique, Character-Values-based approach to building and sustaining a healthy organizational culture that can lead to success and high performance. It is distinguished by four Character Values: Respect, Integrity, Compassion, and Courage.

> "Visionary companies tend to have only a few core values, usually between four and six for only a few values can be truly core. These are values so fundamental and deeply held that they will be changed seldom, if ever… Organizations with enduring success have core values that don't change. Core values are authentic, sacrosanct and distinctive."[33]
> —Jim Collins and Jerry Porras

These are Values that are brought to life in the behaviours and actions distinctive to a Character Culture. The Values are interdependent and are realized in one or more of the character and competence behaviours that lead to high trust. Lencioni describes such values as "permission-to-play values" and warns that they must be delineated to the core. Otherwise, he says "they are generic and non-specific and become diluted and meaningless."

It is noted that the seminal work completed by the Character Community Foundation of York Region, which is mentioned by Gene in this book, outline eleven character attributes: respect, responsibility, honesty, integrity, compassion, courage, inclusiveness, fairness, optimism, perseverance and initiative. Character Culture definitions of respect, integrity, compassion and courage encompass behaviours reflecting the additional seven attributes.

The magnitude of these four Character Values in creating transparency and enabling an organization to become healthy cannot be underestimated. They are reflected in five interdependent and mutually supporting Pillars: Create Clarity, Commit to Accountability, Coach for Performance, Cultivate Collegiality, and Collaborate for Results. These guiding principles are illustrated through essential actions and behaviours, and together provide a foundation for building a Character-Values-based Culture.

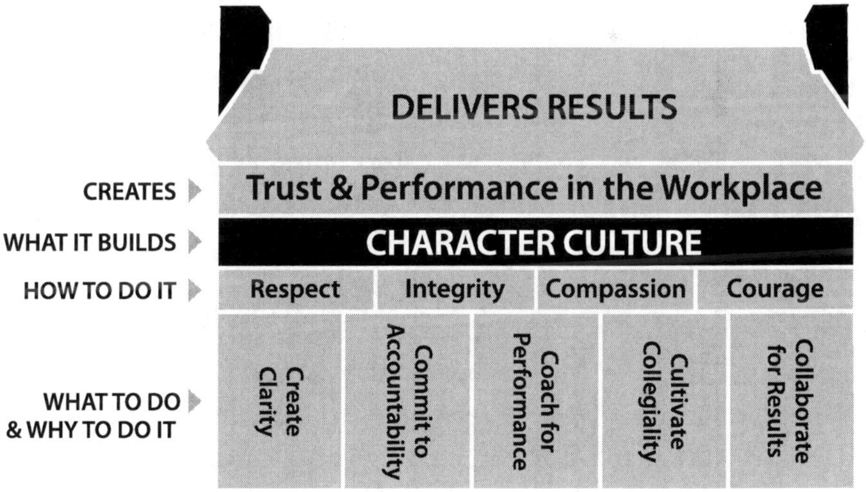

Four Values: The Heart of a Character Culture

The four Character Values are the core convictions that everyone in a Character Culture possesses about *how* they must behave, speak, interact, and contribute in order to fulfill the organization's mission and purpose. They provide a touchstone about the way people not only conduct themselves, but also treat each other at work.

> "Having a statement of values has become common, so the issue is not whether a set of words called 'values' exists somewhere in the company. Adhering to institutional logic makes the regular articulation of values core to the company's work. The CEOs of companies I studied, whether headquartered in the U.S., Mexico, the UK, India, or Japan, allocated considerable resources and their own time to breathing new life into longstanding values statements, engaging managers at many levels in the institutional task of communicating values. The point was not the words themselves, but the process of nurturing a dialogue that would keep social purpose at the forefront of everyone's mind and ensure that employees use the organizational values as a guide for business decisions."[37]
> —Rosabeth Moss Kanter

These are essential values that are "living" and "breathing." Rather than forgotten words on documents or writing on a wall, these are the values that are continuously discussed and/or referenced, strived for, and acted on every day.

Lencioni puts it this way, "More than anything else, values are critical because they define the company's personality. They provide employees with clarity about how to behave."[34] To this, Rosabeth Moss Kanter would add, "Everyone owns them, and the values become embedded in tasks, goals, and performance standards."[35]

These core values are the heart of what organizations consider important. They are as Kotter puts it "the standards set for what people view as 'good,' what quality means, what defines excellence. They are 'what matters most to us.'"[36]

The four "leading" Character Values that are at the heart of a Character Culture are Respect, Integrity, Compassion, and Courage. They are "leading" Values because they represent characteristics that hold the greatest promise for bringing about the high trust, which organizations need to become and remain healthy, and in turn, achieve success.

Character Value One: Respect

Respectful behaviour is civil, dignified, positive, and inclusive.

Over the years, in training sessions and individual coaching conversations there is a theme: people want to be treated respectfully and when they are not, there is a risk of losing their true engagement. In spite of "Respect" being posted on many foyer walls, respectful behaviours are typically neither defined nor living within the organization. The Character Culture Framework defines respectful behaviour. As you read in the quotes, there is interplay between the Values and indeed the Pillars as well.

> "Respect refers to either explicit or implicit expressions of another person's value."[38]
> —Teresa Amabile and Steven Kramer

So, to stay/say more on this note/point—respect is the fundamental belief that everyone in the organization is equal as humans, and deserving of civil treatment and opportunities to become engaged. This value is reflected in actions and behaviours that are dignified, positive, and inclusive.

Unconditional positive regard, a term believed to have been coined by humanist, Carl Rogers, provides another way of thinking about respect. Positive regard involves caring about others, in both their professional and personal capacities. Knowing that others care, reduces one's sense of vulnerability, strengthens social affiliation, and invites reciprocal regard. Those who demonstrate personal regard are considered most likely to be trustworthy.

> "The four major nourishers that fuel inner work life and progress by infusing the work with greater meaning are: respect, encouragement, emotional support, and affiliation."[39]
> —Teresa Amabile and Steven Kramer

Amabile and Kramer, offer another perspective on respect. In their research, they identify respect as a major "nourisher" that fuels inner work life and progress by infusing the work with meaning. They found that "respectful behaviours include recognition and acknowledgement of efforts, valuing ideas and suggestions, dealing with people honestly, and showing basic civility."[40]

The impact of respect in La Maison du Parc is that every person working there will know how to behave civilly in a dignified, positive and inclusive manner. The risk of "disengagement" will be reduced and engagement increased.

Character Value Two: Integrity

Behaving with integrity means being honest, responsible, fair, and consistent.

People want to work for, and with, honest people. The days of "profit only" are gone. The impact on people, society, and the environment is too significant to close our eyes and pretend that shareholder return is enough. The tired excuse "it's what our shareholders want us to do," can no longer justify destruction on any level. At the same time, not-for-profit organizations must honestly achieve meaningful results in order to behave with integrity. Integrity is doing the "right thing."

> "When you consistently demonstrate inner congruence to your belief system and to principles, you inspire trust in both professional and personal relationships."[41]
> —Stephen M. R. Covey

On an individual level, integrity means honesty, but for Covey, honesty means more than telling the truth. It also means "leaving the right impression." Covey argues that because integrity comes from the same Latin root word as the words integrated and integer, a person has integrity when there is no gap between intent and behaviour. He concludes this behaviour adds up to "congruence." People who are congruent, he maintains, "act in harmony with their deepest values and beliefs. They walk the talk."

Covey expands the conventional definition of integrity to include humility. He clarifies that being humble doesn't mean being weak, reticent, or self-effacing. Instead, it means standing firm on principle even in the face of opposition and putting it ahead of self.

At La Maison du Parc, Claire wants to act with integrity as an individual and as leader, and also wants the organization as a whole to have integrity. The Value of Integrity is one more piece of the puzzle to support trustworthy behaviour on the part of leaders and everyone in the organization.

Character Value Three: Compassion

Being compassionate means listening actively, showing empathy, and being caring towards others.

We spend a lot of time at work. No one will debate whether it is better to work in an atmosphere they enjoy versus one they can't stand. It is also better for our physical health to be in a positive environment than a negative one. The behaviours associated with Compassion focus on understanding, caring, and kindness. Many years ago, when I entered the workforce, those concepts were perceived as weak and unacceptable. "Emotion" was left at the door. Now we realize that trust, engagement, and passion for our work are emotions—and these emotions are required for a high performance workplace.

> "... simply acknowledging people's sorrows and frustrations—as well as their joys—can do much to alleviate the negative and amplify the positive emotions."[42]
>
> Empathy is even better than simple acknowledgement—an empathetic word can go a long way toward easing a person's mind and allowing him to get back to the task at hand."[43]
>
> —Teresa Amabile and Steven Kramer

Specifically, to ensure these concepts are behavioural, the Character Value of compassion encompasses empathy and caring. Empathy, defined as the ability to see situations from another's perspective, regardless of whether or not you have experienced what they are experiencing, stands out as foundational to human kindness and consideration.

Covey's fifth habit, "seek first to understand and then to be understood,"[44] is key to communication. For him, it implies learning to rise above your own autobiography and get into the heads and hearts of other people. It involves empathic listening and sensitivity to the situation before attempting to be understood or to influence others, or to make decisions.

> Compassion "can move you to gently place your hand on a co-worker's arm, as you absorb her recounting of the difficulties her family is now enduring. Indeed, the latest evidence suggests that compassionate responding like this is just as natural, just as hard-wired, and just as beneficial to our species as is our evolved instinct to recoil from burning sensations and other forms of physical pain."[45]
> —Barbara Fredrickson

Amabile and Kramer make direct links between compassion and "emotional support," one of the four nourishers of inner work life they say contributes and/or leads to progress. Emotions, they explain, constitute one of the three essential components of inner work life (the others are perceptions/thoughts and motivations/drive). People feel more connected to others at work when their emotions are validated.

In yet another point of view about compassion, psychologist Barbara Fredrickson, author of *Love 2.0: How Our Supreme Emotion Affects Everything We Feel, Think, Do, and Become,* draws on recent science to strongly suggest that love and compassion can be one and the same. "Compassion *is* love," she implies, with the explanation that compassion "flowers when you recognize some kind of physical or emotional pain within the other person."

Claire isn't naïve enough to believe that everyone is going to love everyone else. What she hopes for is a healthy, positive workplace—even if people don't like something about each other, they will still treat each other compassionately.

Character Value Four: Courage

Being courageous means speaking up, hearing feedback, taking initiative, and optimistically persevering.

> "Courage is the first of the human qualities because it is a quality which guarantees all the others."
> —Winston Churchill

Many times over the years people have asked themselves, "Why didn't I speak up?" Because speaking up can be risky business. Especially speaking "truth to power." "If I speak up there may well be a negative consequence," or "Speaking up may well affect my future." These are common beliefs. There is much more opportunity for us to tell the truth to each other and that truth telling will benefit all concerned, including the organization.

Covey has argued that the fourth Character Value of Courage is implied in the value of integrity. Although this is reasonable, in the Character Culture it stands alone as one of the four Character Values to signal its importance. It calls attention to the boldness and fearlessness needed to confront the challenge of staying true to the beliefs and assumptions that underpin the Character Culture.

> "You will never do anything in this world without courage. It is the greatest quality of the mind next to honour."
> —Aristotle

Courage signals the significance of doing the right thing, about remaining optimistic and confident in the face of challenging circumstances. Those who have courage believe that defeat is a temporary setback, that its causes are confined to a single case or challenge.

Courage also calls for resilience. Fredrickson describes resilient people as "emotionally agile." In her view, resilience means "meeting adversity with clear eyes, superbly attuned to the nuances of ever-changing circumstances."[46]

Claire knows that La Maison will improve if she and the team have the information they need to make the right decisions. If information is muted, diluted, or distorted, the organization is

"Resilient people are more hopeful, more excited to rise up to challenges, more appreciative of their many blessings."[47]
—Barbara Fredrickson

at risk. Even though it may be difficult to hear perspectives that are different from initial intentions or are bluntly worded, it is better to gather as much data as possible.

Five Pillars: Guiding Principles and Essential Character and Competence Behaviours

The Five Pillars provide the "what and why": what leaders and all staff must do to create an effective organization and why the behaviours are significant.

The five interrelated and interdependent Pillars which provide the foundations of the Framework are:

- Pillar One: Create Clarity
- Pillar Two: Commit to Accountability
- Pillar Three: Coach for Performance
- Pillar Four: Cultivate Collegiality
- Pillar Five: Collaborate for Results

An overarching and unique guiding principle sets the standard for each Pillar. The essential behaviours that specify expectations related to leaders and to all employees integrate dimensions associated with the character and competence needed to build high trust.

The behaviours are those that both research and practice identify as critical and unique to a Character Culture. They are both a resource and a reference point that provide a common language and contribute to a shared understanding about what is expected of everyone in the organization. They become a touchstone for growth and development on a continuum of performance.

Given that the culture of every organization has its own personality, the behaviours specified here may be tailored to reflect the uniqueness of organizations across diverse contexts. In addition, the expression of these behaviours within the organization will vary.

Pillar One: Create Clarity

Everyone knows and understands organizational purpose, goals, progress, and results.

Would you be surprised to know that many people work very hard, but deep down feel that their efforts result in very little? Either they are "going through the motions" and fulfilling a process instead of creating a meaningful outcome, or the organization's purpose is so vague that it is irrelevant to them. Engagement results, in part, from a sense of purpose. Clarity supports and defines the desired end results and the steps along the way.

CREATE CLARITY
The sample behaviour, "leaders model and promote the Character Values," reflects all the Character Values and at the same time, integrates competencies such as developing relationships and clarifying expectations.

Patrick Lencioni stands out among educators in making a case for both creating and communicating for clarity. In his view, "clarity is the antidote to anxiety," and must be "the preoccupation of the effective leader," so that everyone in the organization understands what is expected and knows where to get input and information when it is needed.

Marcus Buckingham likewise identifies clarity as key to organizational and individual success. The four points of clarity he identifies are:

1. Who do we serve?
2. What is our core strength?
3. What is our core score? (leading indicator(s) of success)
4. What actions can we take today?

Lencioni has similarly identified six simple but critical questions:

1. Why do we exist?
2. How do we behave?
3. What do we do?
4. How will we succeed?
5. What is most important, right now?
6. Who must do that?

For Lencioni, clarity is all about achieving alignment. And so he goes a step further arguing that once clarity and alignment are established, the next step is to over communicate. "Over communication" means communicating answers to the critical questions, "clearly, repeatedly, enthusiastically, and repeatedly (and that's not a typo)."

> "By far the most effective way to turn fear into confidence is to be clear; to define the future in such vivid terms, through your actions, words, images, pictures, heroes and scores, that we can all see where you, and thus we, are headed ..."[48]
> —Marcus Buckingham

Finally, he stresses that, for an organization to remain healthy over time, its leaders must establish systems to reinforce clarity in every process that involves people. "Every policy, every activity should be designed to remind employees what is really most important."[50]

Communicating with clarity leads to the transparency needed to bring about healthy organizations. In *Transparency: How Leaders Create a Culture of Candour*, Bennis, Goleman, and O'Toole contend that transparency encompasses candour, integrity, honesty, ethics, clarity, full disclosure, legal compliance, and more, and allows everyone in the organization to deal fairly with each other.

> "When it comes to reinforcing clarity, there is no such thing as too much communication."[49]
> —Patrick Lencioni

A culture of candour is the free flow of information within an organization, and between the organization and its many stakeholders, including the public.

Without transparency, people don't believe what others in their organization say, including their leaders.

> "For any institution, the flow of information is akin to a central nervous system: the organization's capacity to compete, solve problems, innovate, meet challenges, and achieve goals— its intelligence…"[51]
> —Warren Bennis, Daniel Goleman, and James O'Toole

Gene reminded Claire of the focus and transparency of a hockey game. If every person doesn't know what La Maison is trying to achieve, the progress towards the outcome and how their individual contribution affects that outcome, then the restaurant won't succeed. It's that simple.

Pillar Two: Commit To Accountability

Everyone commits to the success of the organization by fulfilling their commitments, taking responsibility for their behaviour, and striving for excellence.

Accountability is a word I hear a lot. People often ask me: "how do I hold someone accountable?" "Is it just up to me as the leader? I don't want people telling on each other." "What do I do when someone has been here years and years and suddenly seems to be coasting?" "How do I do this without causing conflict?" The answer is we all share in the issue of accountability and there are several pieces to this puzzle. Clarity is the first Pillar, as people need to know what they are required to do and why; not to the point where individuality is lost … just the opposite. Fresh thinking and approaches are critical. Having said that, there are still basics that are required. Our research demonstrates that the Character Pillars and Values are the basics. Understanding the foundational expectations provides everyone the opportunity to hold

> **COMMIT TO ACCOUNTABILITY**
> The sample behaviour, "leaders are responsible to one another about commitments and behaviours," reflects all four Character Values, and also integrates competencies that include taking responsibility for results and helping to get things done.

> "Individuals committed to a vision beyond their self-interest find they have energy not available when pursuing narrower goals as will organizations that tap this level of commitment."[52]
> —Peter Senge

themselves and everyone else accountable for reasonable, effective behaviour.

"Accountability" sometimes carries negative connotations because it is often mistakenly regarded as a system of strict oversight, rewards, and punishments. On the contrary, in the business environment, accountability should be a collaborative model of responsibilities shared by both leaders and their staff. Effectively implemented and executed, accountability functions in a positive, constructive manner, and, with the appropriate means of feedback and development, represents a source of inspiration for all.

A framework of accountability should not, and must not be a harsh set of practices. Instead, accountability should be set in a collaborative context that fosters a stimulating atmosphere of enthusiasm and ambition. It should create and convey an air of opportunity throughout the organization that includes occasions for coaching, mentoring, and leading, and for everyone to excel, achieve, and benefit both personally and professionally.

> "Peer-to-peer accountability is the primary and most effective source of accountability on a leadership team."[53]
> —Patrick Lencioni

Although Lencioni would agree that accountability structures should not be bureaucratic and inhibit independence and self-direction, he cautions that team leaders and team members need to be held accountable, "if a team is going to stick to its decisions and accomplish its goals." In his view, "at its core, accountability is about having the courage to confront someone about their deficiencies and then to stand in the moment and deal with their reaction, which may not be pleasant."[55]

While Claire struggled with Paul's behaviour, she did ultimately clarify what was expected of him. Paul chose to not be part of La Maison or the leadership team. Claire accepted his decision. Paul's case was obvious; he quit. Where it is more difficult is when people know what is expected and stay. That is when "Commit to Accountability" kicks in. Peers and leaders must be honest with people and hold them accountable for their choice... in a respectful, appropriate, fair manner.

The other piece of the accountability puzzle is the requirement for a report card or scorecard. This tool builds on the Pillar of Create Clarity. A good scorecard is simple, brief, understandable, up-to-date and meaningful to everyone. A living document. Claire, with Gene's help, quickly ensured the development of an initial scorecard to create concrete, immediate goals and up-to-date, properly communicated information. This process helps everyone know for **what** they are accountable.

> "To hold someone accountable is to care about them enough to risk having them blame you for pointing out their deficiencies."[54]
> —Patrick Lencioni

"Measurement is the first step that leads to control and eventually to improvement. If you can't measure something, you can't understand it. If you can't understand it, you can't control it. If you can't control it, you can't improve it."[56]

Pillar Three: Coach For Performance

Everyone supports the ongoing development of others with a focus on maximizing individual potential and organizational performance.

"Who is accountable for performance?" we asked in Commit to Accountability. The answer is—everyone. The concept is that we are all responsible to help each other be the best we can be, at least within the behaviours of the Character Culture Framework. The goal is not for all leaders, or indeed staff, to be certified executive coaches like Gene. The expectation is that everyone possesses skill in terms of clarifying expectations, offering positive and developmental feedback, and listening to others as laid out in the Framework.

Most certainly, an underutilized and powerful skill is, to quote Ken Blanchard, "catching people doing something right." Years after he and co-author Spencer Johnson penned that powerful statement in the *One Minute Manager,* there is still much we can improve in letting people know what progress they are making and the impact of their contributions.

The multi-year study conducted by Amabile and Kramer, which tracked the day-to-day activities, emotions and motivational levels of hundreds of knowledge workers in a wide variety of settings, leaves no doubt but that the top motivator of performance is "progress."

COACH FOR PROGRESS
The sample behaviour, "leaders engage in, encourage and promote open and honest communication," reflects all four Character Values and also integrates competencies that include developing people and listening first.

To coach for performance begins with models provided by leaders in organizations. Marcus Buckingham has found that, in most organizations, commitment to each employee's success appears to be driven less by logic than by intuition and instinct. Instead he argues that great leaders must have an ability to derive satisfaction from seeing tiny increments of growth in someone else. This talent, he states, is commonly known as the "coaching instinct."

In the people-oriented Character Culture, effective leaders ensure that their employees transfer their skills and interests to practical performance in order to reach their full potential. They go the further step of making it possible for employees to develop the coaching instinct—the concept of wanting each individual to flourish while maintaining an overview of the organization and its purpose in the backs of their minds.

"When it comes to giver-cultures, the role-modelling lesson here is a powerful one: if you want it, go and give it."[57]
—Adam Grant

Confirming that making progress is a key motivator of performance is good news for organizations, as it is largely within their control. Leaders have within their reach, influence over events and working conditions that can facilitate progress. What does "Coaching for Performance" look like in the "giver-culture" that a Character Culture embodies? First, a leader's or colleague's own enthusiasm can help increase motivation for the work. Leaders can cultivate a climate of helpfulness. Leaders can also facilitate progress more directly, say Amabile and Kramer, simply by rolling up sleeves and pitching in.

La Maison du Parc is a small organization. You have seen and will continue to see the leaders be very "hands-on." In large organizations, one of the risks is the distance between the leaders and the front-line workers. It is fascinating to watch the surprise expressed by leaders in the popular T.V. series, *Undercover Boss* when they work side by side with staff. The five Pillars, including Coach for Performance, highlight the importance of knowing what is going on in our organizations in order to support success.

Pillar Four: Cultivate Collegiality

Everyone contributes to an enjoyable workplace where they feel safe, engaged and valued.

Feeling safe is an emotion. Feelings of safety emerge when you trust the people around you to behave in a healthy, reasonable manner. Engagement is also an emotion. The behaviours in the Pillars and Values support a healthy, engaging workplace. Feeling valued is a key piece of the puzzle and overlaps with several other puzzle pieces, including Coaching for Performance. Even if we make a mistake, we can still feel valued. How we, and others, deal with it, is key. The word used to summarize a safe, engaging workplace is collegiality.

Amabile and Kramer define collegiality as, "any action that contributes to team cohesiveness: it is what team members demonstrate when they support each other interpersonally, act as if they are all part of the same team and work effort, and show that they care about how well the team functions."

The four nourishers these researchers identify—respect, encouragement, emotional support, and affiliation—together fuel inner work life and progress by infusing the work with greater meaning.

Affiliation they argue best describes how collegiality emerges. Affiliation refers to actions that develop bonds of mutual trust, appreciation, and even affection with coworkers, and is the most obvious way in which people feed the human connection at work.

> "When we care about the people we work with, we want to succeed for them. When our colleagues become a kind of family to us, work can take on new meaning in our lives. Human connections really can inspire people to 'go the extra mile for the team.'"[58]
>
> —Teresa Amabile and Steven Kramer

When people enjoy each other, they assert, there are fewer and milder interpersonal conflicts that can negatively impact the work. Building bonds between team members can also improve the flow of ideas and increase collaboration. Generally, the more closely bonded team members are to one another, the better inner work life will be across a team and the greater their progress.

Behaviours associated with affiliation include doing something explicitly for the sake of the team (rather than simply the work or the project); doing something to increase emotional bonding within the team; having fun with teammates at work or outside of work; and demonstrated pride, affection or warmth for a teammate or the team as a whole. (Amabile and Kramer)

Our story ends with a team celebration. The staff is marking a milestone. They are also permanently honouring their founder, Charles. The moment is one of good feelings supported by their specialty: good food and drink. Gene and Claire know that it is important to allow staff an opportunity to enjoy the building, their creativity and each other's company.

Pillar Five: Collaborate For Results

Everyone works collaboratively to improve the organization and achieve strategic goals.

Collaboration is an often-heard word—especially in the workplace, but clients tell me that collaborating is challenging. We are now working and collaborating in different ways, in different languages, with different technologies. Despite its challenges, collaboration is a good thing—or better said, good collaboration for concrete results is a good thing.

COLLABORATE FOR INNOVATION
The sample behaviour, "leaders compromise on individual departmental agendas for the benefit of the organization," reflects all four Character Values and also integrates competencies that include building teams.

Most leaders of the 21st century believe that company-wide collaboration is essential for successful strategy implementation. They are right in seeing collaboration's tremendous potential.

While this may be the accepted wisdom, the Character Culture envisioned draws on the cautions of Morton Hansen, author of *Collaboration: How Leaders Avoid the Traps, Build Common Ground, and Reap Big Results,* who argues that there is a right way and a wrong way to collaborate. For him, the idea of disciplined collaboration can be summed up in one phrase: "The leadership practice of properly assessing when to collaborate (and when not to) and instilling in people both the willingness and the ability to collaborate when required."[60]

The whole idea of collaboration is not only to tear down silos and get people to work together. To be worthwhile, Hansen says, "Collaboration must generate results. It must be disciplined and effective. Disciplined collaboration will amplify the results each individual would have attained, whereas poor collaboration can actually end up being worse than no collaboration at all."[61]

> "Although the collaborative imperative is a hallmark of today's business environment, the challenge is not to cultivate more collaboration. Rather, it is to cultivate the right collaboration, so that we can achieve the great things not possible when we work alone."[59]
> —Morton Hansen

Amabile and Kramer draw direct linkages between collaboration and collegiality. In their research they identified seven major catalysts that promote and support work: setting clear goals, allowing autonomy, providing resources, giving enough time—but not too much, helping with the work, learning from problems and successes, allowing ideas to flow. Among these catalysts "helping with the work" calls for collaboration.

In modern organizations, people need each other; almost everyone works interdependently. Employees left entirely to their own devices, without any assistance or support from someone else, accomplish very little—they need help. Help can take many forms, from providing needed information, to brainstorming with a colleague, to collaborating with someone who is struggling. Employees become dejected when help is inaccessible.

Relational or altruistic motivation arises from the need to connect with, and help other people. The camaraderie that comes from collaborating with congenial colleagues can drive us in our work, and so can the belief that our work has real value to a person, a group, or society at large.

> "Positive emotions fuel people's motivation, which in turn drives performance along four key dimensions:
> 1. Creativity—ability to come up with novel and useful ideas
> 2. Productivity
> 3. Commitment to the work, and
> 4. Collegiality—contributions to team cohesiveness."[62]
>
> —Teresa Amabile and Steven Kramer

Everyone at La Maison du Parc needs everyone else in order to achieve their purpose. They must truly become a high performing, effective team to be successful. A Character Culture will help them achieve that goal.

Part Three

The Tools:
The Character Culture Focus

The Character Culture Roadmap

Roadmap for Transforming to Character Culture

This graphic outlines the key steps in transforming to a Character Culture.

STEPS	ACTIONS
Vision for Culture	Senior leader commits to a vision for transforming to a Character Culture
Engage Workforce	Leaders and then entire workforce are enrolled in vision and process Communication plan created to keep everyone informed at every step
Create a Benchmark	Assess the current culture by administering (customized) Character Culture Survey
Develop goals and plan to achieve Organizational Purpose	1. Celebrate & leverage strengths. 2. Develop a plan to: • create systemic alignment • train & coach as required • establish milestones • measure progress
Provide Training and Coaching	Train and coach as required
Reassess and Refine	Measure & celebrate progress. Refine plan to meet new goals

What Drives Performance

How Character Culture drives performance. The culture is intentional rather than reactive.

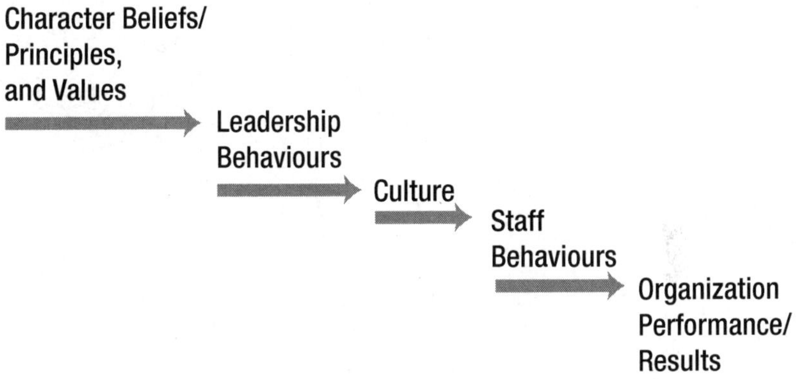

Character Culture Framework – 5 Pillars

The Character Culture Framework is designed to build and sustain the trust needed to bring out the best in each person to realize the organizational purpose and achieve goals. ***The five Pillars support organizational effectiveness.***

5 Pillars	Create Clarity	Commit to Accountability
Guiding Principles **Why this Pillar is important…**	Everyone knows and understands organizational purpose, goals, progress, and results.	Everyone commits to the success of the organization by fulfilling their commit-ments, taking responsibility for their behaviour, and striving for excellence.
Sample Leadership behaviours **Leaders...**	Clarify organizational purpose, significance and impact Establish performance expectations Link assignments to organizational purpose Provide concrete organizational information on goals, productivity, progress and results Model and promote the Character Values Are transparent and consistent in decision-making Incorporate Values into human resource systems	Hold themselves and others accountable for goals, progress and results Assess staff performance in relation to organizational goals, progress and results Assess staff behaviour in relation to the Character Culture Framework Provide appropriate tools, resources Foster and support autonomy where appropriate Are responsible to one another about commitments and behaviours
Sample behaviours for everyone (including leaders) **Everyone...**	Supports the five Pillars Models/practices Character Values Requests input/information when needed Understands what is expected	Assesses impact of their words and actions on others and on organizational goals, progress and results Self-manages by identifying intentions, thoughts and feelings which manifest in behaviour Is open to and strives for continuous improvement

Character Culture Framework Pillars—Creating the what and why foundation of a Character Culture.

Coach for Performance	Cultivate Collegiality	Collaborate for Results
Everyone supports the ongoing development of others with a focus on maximizing individual potential and organization performance.	Everyone contributes to an enjoyable workplace where they feel safe, engaged, and valued.	Everyone works collaboratively to improve the organization and achieve strategic goals.
Engage in, encourage and promote open and honest feedback in all directions Hold regular one-on-one meetings with leader, peers and direct reports Coach on performance by inquiring about intentions, thoughts and feelings which manifest in behaviour Acknowledge and celebrate progress and results Provide ongoing developmental opportunities	Establish and maintain a trusting workplace climate that promotes engagement, inclusion, caring and a sense of belonging Create awareness of the significance of body language and tone of voice in communication Clarify that technology (email, texts, voice mail etc.) is used in a careful manner. Face to face conversations are required if there is a sensitive issue	(Senior Leaders) support the "first team – the senior leadership team," as fully as their departmental teams Compromise on departmental agendas for the benefit of the organization Provide the structure and conditions to promote working together in cross-functional teams Create a simple, open to all staff, system for encouraging and harvesting innovative ideas
Offers feedback according to the agreed upon workplace protocols Communicates to leader and/or appropriate parties any opportunities to improve the organization Helps others to build their capacity to problem solve in challenging situations	Speaks up when there are opportunities for, and barriers to, collegiality and engagement Develops successful working relationships with all parties by adapting the Character Values Respects and supports diversity	Contributes to the success of the organization by taking the initiative in developing collaborative relationships with all parties, including the greater community Offers innovative suggestions for improving the organization using the system for harvesting innovative ideas

Character Culture Framework – Character Values

The Character Culture Framework integrates character and competence behaviours that are essential ingredients of trust. ***Character Values clarify how people behave in a Character Culture to develop and sustain high trust.***

Respect	Integrity
Respectful behaviour is civil, dignified, positive and inclusive.	*Behaving with integrity means being honest, responsible, fair, and consistent.*
I practice good etiquette by saying hello, goodbye, please, and thank you	I keep promises and commitments
I am punctual and let others know if and why I will be late	I tell the truth and speak from my "I" to take responsibility for words and actions
I ask people for time rather than interrupting	I ask rather than speculate on motives, thoughts, and feelings of others
I ensure others have ample opportunity to speak in conversations and meetings	I take responsibility for, and learn from, my mistakes
I am committed to the success of others, including offering developmental feedback	I strive for a win-win in all circumstances
I speak positively about my organization and colleagues	I speak directly to the person when there is a problem
I celebrate the progress and success of others	I protect the privacy of others
I use inclusive and thoughtful language and approaches with others	I explain the rationale for decisions and requests where possible
I value and learn from the differences between us	I am aware of my moods and adjust them to be collegial, collaborative, and constructive
I involve others in decision-making, discussions, and events where appropriate	I contribute to our community and society

Compassion	Courage
Being compassionate means listening actively, showing empathy, and being caring towards others.	*Being courageous means speaking up, hearing feedback, taking initiative, and optimistically persevering.*
I listen actively and openly in order to fully hear and understand what is being communicated	I state my perspective/ opinion when it seems helpful and/or is requested
I check for understanding to help ensure that I understand what others are saying and feeling	I engage in courageous conversations when appropriate and refrain from gossip
I show empathy by putting myself in the other person's shoes	I listen to feedback offered to me and discuss how to modify/adjust my approach if this is needed
I reflect the message and emotion (acknowledgement) in challenging or significant conversations	I reflect on how to improve my performance
I offer positive feedback in a generous, timely, specific manner	I am clear in my response whether the answer is "yes" or "no"
I offer developmental feedback in a constructive, open, inquiring manner that leads to a solution	I am authentic by considering my intentions, thoughts, and feelings and ensuring alignment with my behaviour
I separate the person from the issue when offering feedback	I am always assessing how to do things better and more effectively
I ask rather than tell	I go the extra mile to get the job done
I describe my own experiences as a way of providing support rather than offering advice	I seek solutions to setbacks and obstacles
I am considerate and kind	I do what is right versus popular

Chartering Culture Advisory Success Team (CAST)

Teams work in different ways—the key is to create an explicit charter. Here are headings and questions to help get your chartering effort rolling.

Purpose of CAST:
What is the role of the team? The overarching purpose? How is the CAST determined?

Project Outcomes:
What are your deliverables? Timelines? What are the costs involved in CAST?

Measurement: How will you measure the success of the CAST?

Timelines: What other timelines are applicable?

Ground rules:
Who is the leader(s)? What is their role? How will you work together? Who is in charge of monitoring the budget (costs)? How will you handle conflict? How will decisions be made? How will you celebrate progress?

Progress:
How will you acknowledge progress? What will you do if there is a lack of progress?

Barriers:
What barriers may arise? How will they be handled? What will you do if unforeseen barriers arise?

Accountability:
What is each person responsible for? How do team members hold each other accountable for their commitments? What is the role of the leader regarding accountability?

CAST Meetings and Membership:
In person meetings? Where and when do you meet? How are minutes handled? Email communication? Who is copied on emails?

How long does this team continue? How will you evolve to a new team?

Will you open meetings to other staff members?

Communication with Staff:
How will you communicate with staff? What will you communicate? When? Who is responsible to ensure the communication takes place?

Definitions

Character Culture	A Character Culture fosters a healthy workplace where there is high trust, authentic engagement, and sustained focus on organizational purpose and results.
Character Culture Framework	The Character Culture Framework provides people with a clear picture of what a Character Culture looks like at all levels of an organization. It describes what people do (competence) and how they work together (character) irrespective of roles and responsibilities. It is a resource that organizations can use to foster a healthy workplace characterized by high trust, authentic engagement, and sustained focus on organizational purpose.
Character Culture Pillars	The five Character Culture Pillars: Create Clarity, Commit to Accountability, Coach for Performance, Cultivate Collegiality, and Collaborate for Results are the guiding principles of a Character Culture. They inform "what to do."
Character Culture Values	The four Character Values: Respect, Integrity, Compassion, and Courage inform "how to do what you are doing." The Pillars and Values join forces to create a Character Culture.
Character	Two dictionary definitions: "The mental and moral qualities distinctive to an individual." — *New Oxford Dictionary of English*. "A composite of good moral qualities typical of moral excellence and firmness blended with resolution, self-discipline, high ethics, force and judgement." —Webster's 3rd New *International Dictionary of the English Language* Unabridged 2002. Which lead to the definition in *Leadership by Engagement*: "Character is the whole person, everything we believe, say and do, in our own unique way."

References

1. Webster's English Dictionary. http://www.merriam-webster.com/dictionary/character.
2. Webster's *3rd New International Dictionary of the English Language*, Unabridged 2002.
3. Gerard Seijts, Jeffrey Gandz, Mary Crossan and Mark Reno, "Character: The Essence of Leadership," *Developing Leaders* 10 (2013): 16, http://www.ivey.uwo.ca/research/leadership/research/topics/leadership-skills/practitioner-articles/character-essence.pdf.
4. Ibid.
5. Ibid., 12.
6. Jeffrey Gandz, "Good leadership begins with solid values," *The Globe and Mail* (September 15, 2011): http://www.theglobeandmail.com/report-on-business/careers/careers-leadership/gandz-good-leadership-begins-with-solid-values/article556911/?page=all.
7. Dov Seidman, *How: Why How We Do Anything Means Everything* (New Jersey: John Wiley & Sons, Inc., 2007), 136.
8. Megan Tschannen-Moran, *Trust Matters* (San Francisco: Jossey-Bass, 2004), 18-33.
9. Ibid.
10. Dov Seidman, *How: Why How We Do Anything Means Everything* (New Jersey: John Wiley & Sons, Inc., 2007), 172.
11. Gerard Seijts, Jeffrey Gandz, Mary Crossan and Mark Reno, "Character: The Essence of Leadership," *Developing Leaders* 10 (2013): 15, http://www.ivey.uwo.ca/research/leadership/research/topics/leadership-skills/practitioner-articles/character-essence.pdf.
12. Ibid., 15.

13. Warren Buffet, "Berkshire Hathaway Inc.," Shareholder Letters, http://www.berkshirehathaway.com/letters/letters.html.

14. Dov Seidman, *How: Why How We Do Anything Means Everything* (New Jersey: John Wiley & Sons, Inc., 2007), 159.

15. Stephen Covey, *The Speed of Trust* (New York: Free Press, 2006).

16. Mary Crossan, Jeffrey Gandz and Gerard Seijts, "Developing Leadership Character," *Ivey Business Journal* (Feb. 2012), http://www.iveybusinessjournal.com/topics/leadership/developing-leadership-character#.UildQTZm_pQ.

17. Patrick Lencioni, *The Advantage: Why Organizational Health Trumps Everything Else in Business* (San Francisco: Jossey-Bass, 2012).

18. John P. Kotter, *Leading Change* (New York: Harvard Business School Press, 1996), 148.

19. Edgar Schein, *Organizational Culture and Leadership* (San Francisco: Jossey-Bass, 2010), 18.

20. Dov Seidman, *How: Why How We Do Anything Means Everything* (New Jersey: John Wiley & Sons, Inc., 2007), 218.

21. Patrick Lencioni, *The Advantage: Why Organizational Health Trumps Everything Else in Business* (San Francisco: Jossey-Bass, 2012).

22. Dov Seidman, *How: Why How We Do Anything Means Everything* (New Jersey: John Wiley & Sons, Inc., 2007), 219.

23. Paul Rogers, Paul Meehan and Scott Tanner, "Building a Winning Culture," Bain & Company, Insights (August 2006), http://www.bain.com/publications/articles/building-winning-culture.aspx.

24. Thomas Peters and Robert Waterman, *In Search of Excellence: Lessons from America's Best-Run Companies* (New York: Harper Row, 1982), 1.

25. Ibid., 76.

26. Teresa Amabile and Steven Kramer, *The Progress Principle: Using Small Wins to Ignite Joy, Enagement, and Creativity at Work* (Boston: Harvard Business School, 2011), 18.

27. Ibid., 3.

28. Ibid., 2.

29. Paul Rogers, Paul Meehan and Scott Tanner, "Building a Winning Culture," Bain & Company, Insights (August 2006),1, http://www.bain.com/publications/articles/building-winning-culture.aspx.

30. Steven Kelman and Sounman Hong, "Harvard Faculty Research Working Paper Series," Harvard Kennedy School (2012), 1.

31. Ibid.

32. Adam Grant, *In the Company of Givers and Takers* (New York: Harvard Business Review, April, 2013), 2.

33. Jim Collins and Jerry Porras, *Built to Last: Successful Habits of Visionary Companies* (New York: Harper Collins, 1994), 74.

34. Patrick Lencioni, *The Advantage: Why Organizational Health Trumps Everything Else in Business* (San Francisco: Jossey-Bass, 2012), 91.

35. Rosabeth Moss Kanter, *How Great Companies Think Differently* (New York: Harvard Business Review, Nov. 2011), 7.

36. John P. Kotter, *Leading Change* (New York: Harvard Business School Press, 1996).

37. Rosabeth Moss Kanter, *How Great Companies Think Differently* (New York: Harvard Business Review, Nov. 2011), 7.

38. Teresa Amabile and Steven Kramer, *The Progress Principle: Using Small Wins to Ignite Joy, Enagement, and Creativity at Work* (Boston: Harvard Business School, 2011), 149.

39. Ibid., 131.

40. Ibid.

41. Stephen Covey, *The Speed of Trust* (New York: Free Press, 2006), 63.

42. Teresa Amabile and Steven Kramer, *The Progress Principle: Using Small Wins to Ignite Joy, Enagement, and Creativity at Work* (Boston: Harvard Business School, 2011), 132.

43. Ibid.

44. Stephen Covey, *The Seven Habits of Highly Effective People* (New York: Free Press, 1989), 237.

45. Barbara Fredrickson, *Love 2.0: How Our Supreme Emotion Affects Everything We Fell, Think, Do, and Become* (New York: Penguin Group, 2013), 142.

46. Ibid.

47. Ibid., 78.

48. Marcus Buckingham, *The One Thing You Need to Know... About Great Managing, Great Leading, and Sustained Individual Success* (New York: Free Press, 2005), 145.

49. Patrick Lencioni, *The Advantage: Why Organizational Health Trumps Everything Else in Business* (San Francisco: Jossey-Bass, 2012), 15.

50. Ibid., 16.

51. Warren Bennis, Daniel Goleman and James O'Toole, *Transparency: How Leaders Create a Culture of Candour* (San Francisco, Jossey-Bass, 2008).

52. Peter Senge, *The Fifth Discipline: The Art and Practice of the Learning Organization* (New York: Doubleday, 1990), 171.

53. Patrick Lencioni, *The Advantage: Why Organizational Health Trumps Everything Else in Business* (San Francisco: Jossey-Bass, 2012), 57
54. Ibid.
55. Ibid.
56. H. James Harrington, http://www.goodreads.com/quotes/632992-measurement-is-the-first-step-that-leads-to-control-and.
57. Adam Grant, *Givers Take All: The Hidden Dimension of Corporate Culture* (New York: McKinsey Quarterly, 2013), 13.
58. Teresa Amabile and Steven Kramer, *The Progress Principle: Using Small Wins to Ignite Joy, Enagement, and Creativity at Work* (Boston: Harvard Business School, 2011), 131.
59. Morton Hansen, *When Internal Collaboration is Bad for Your Company* (New York: Harvard Business Review, 2009), 6-7.
60. Ibid., 15.
61. Ibid. (adapted quote)
62. Teresa Amabile and Steven Kramer, *The Progress Principle: Using Small Wins to Ignite Joy, Enagement, and Creativity at Work* (Boston: Harvard Business School, 2011), 131.

Additional Resources

Character Community of York Region – www.CharacterCommunity.com

Mental Fitness Magazine – www.MentalFitnessMagazine.com

Bibliography

Amabile, Teresa and Steven Kramer. *The Progress Principle: Using Small Wins to Ignite Joy, Enagement, and Creativity at Work*. Boston: Harvard Business School, 2011.

Bennis, Warren, Daniel Goleman and James O'Toole. *Transparency: How Leaders Create a Culture of Candour*. San Francisco: Jossey-Bass, 2008.

Blanchard, Kenneth and Spencer Johnson. *The One Minute Manager*. New York: William Morrow, 1982.

Buckingham, Marcus. *The One Thing You Need to Know... About Great Managing, Great Leading, and Sustained Individual Success*. New York: Free Press, 2005.

Character Community Foundation of York Region. http://www.charactercommunity.com.

Collins, Jim. *Good to Great*. New York: Harper Collins, 2001.

Collins, Jim and Jerry Porras. *Built to Last: Successful Habits of Visionary Companies*. New York: Harper Collins, 1994.

Collins, Jim and Morten T. Hansen. *Great by Choice*. New York: Harper Collins, 2011.

Covey, Stephen. *The Seven Habits of Highly Effective People*. New York: Free Press, 1989.

Covey, Stephen. *The Speed of Trust*. New York: Free Press, 2006.

Fredrickson, Barbara. *Love 2.0: How Our Supreme Emotion Affects Everything We Fell, Think, Do, and Become*. New York: Penguin Group, 2013.

Hansen, Morton. Collaboration: How Leaders Avoid the Traps, Create Unity, and Reap Big Results. Boston: Harvard Business Review Press, 2009.

Kotter, John P. *Leading Change.* New York: Harvard Business School Press, 1996.

Lencioni, Patrick. *The Advantage: Why Organizational Health Trumps Everything Else in Business*. San Francisco: Jossey-Bass, 2012.

Peters, Thomas and Robert H. Waterman Jr. *In Search Of Excellence: Lessons from America's Best-Run Companies*. New York: Harper Row, 1982.

Peterson, Christopher and Martin E. P. Seligman. *Character Strengths and Virtues*. Washington, DC: Oxford University Press, 2004.

Redmond, Kathleen. *Leadership by Engagement*. Toronto: Engagement Publishing, 2009.

Schein, Edgar. *Organizational Culture and Leadership*. San Francisco: Jossey-Bass, 2010.

Senge, Peter. *The Fifth Discipline: The Art and Practice of the Learning Organization*. New York: Doubleday, 1990.

Tschannen-Moran, Megan. *Trust Matters*. San Francisco: Jossey-Bass, 2004.

Permissions

Every attempt has been made to give proper acknowledgement, and access appropriate permissions for quotes. Any oversights are purely unintentional. In the unlikely event something has been missed, please accept our regret and apology, and contact us immediately so we can investigate and rectify as needed.

Publisher's Note

When a gifted author presents an exciting concept such as the Character Culture Framework which you'll discover in *Building a Character Culture*, and combines it with a well told story to provide a captivating and relatable example, we are treated to an accomplished publication such as this. Kathleen's talent lies in the ability to bring together a phenomenal amount of well researched data and create an appealing narrative that outlines just how effective and necessary this model is to create a successful environment in the workplace.

As publisher and editor of *Building a Character Culture for Trust and Results in the Workplace*, it has been an honour to work with Kathleen. Her attention to detail and hands-on approach makes her passion extremely evident, and speaks volumes about her commitment to produce a product that truly delivers in every sense.

Building a Character Culture is the beginning of a dynamic new series you will definitely want to follow. Be sure to watch for Kathleen's next offerings coming soon: *Communicating in a Character Culture*, and *Coaching in a Character Culture*.

Sheri Andrunyk
Publisher, Editor, Author, Speaker & Consultant
Insightful Communications Publishing
I C Publishing… Committed to Quality Content